CW00473081

Happiness

ALSO AVAILABLE FROM BLOOMSBURY

Being and Event, Alain Badiou

Conditions, Alain Badiou

Infinite Thought, Alain Badiou

Logics of Worlds, Alain Badiou

Theoretical Writings, Alain Badiou

Theory of the Subject, Alain Badiou

Anti-Oedipus, Gilles Deleuze

Thousand Plateaus, Gilles Deleuze and Félix Guattari

Molecular Revolution, Félix Guattari

Schizoanalytic Cartographies, Félix Guattari

The Three Ecologies, Félix Guattari

Seeing the Invisible, Michel Henry

After Finitude, Quentin Meillassoux

Time for Revolution, Antonio Negri

Althusser's Lesson, Jacques Rancière

Chronicles of Consensual Times, Jacques Rancière

Mallarmé, Jacques Rancière

Politics of Aesthetics, Jacques Rancière

The Five Senses, Michel Serres

Rome, Michel Serres

Statues, Michel Serres

Art and Fear, Paul Virilio

Negative Horizon, Paul Virilio

Happiness

By Alain Badiou

Translated with foreword by
A. J. Bartlett and Justin Clemens

BLOOMSBURY ACADEMIC
LONDON • NEW YORK • OXFORD • NEW DELHI • SYDNEY

BLOOMSBURY ACADEMIC
Bloomsbury Publishing Plc
50 Bedford Square, London, WC1B 3DP, UK
1385 Broadway, New York, NY 10018, USA

BLOOMSBURY, BLOOMSBURY ACADEMIC and the Diana logo
are trademarks of Bloomsbury Publishing Plc

First published in French as *Métaphysique du bonheur reel*,
Presses Universitaires de France, © Alain Badiou 2015

English translation © Bloomsbury Publishing Plc, 2019

Cover design by Catherine Wood

A catalogue record for this book is available from the British Library.

ISBN: HB: 978-1-4742–7552-1
PB: 978-1-4742–7553-8
ePDF: 978-1-4742–7554-5
eBook: 978-1-4742–7555-2

A catalog record for this book is available from the Library of Congress.

Typeset by Fakenham Prepress Solutions, Fakenham, Norfolk NR21 8NN
Printed and bound in Great Britain

To find out more about our authors and books visit
www.bloomsbury.com and sign up for our newsletters.

Contents

Contents

Acknowledgements

Aside from Alain Badiou himself, the translators would also like to thank Robert Boncado, Bryan Cooke, Lia Hills, Helen Johnson, Isabelle Vodoz and Angela Cullip for their indispensable aid with the preparation of this translation.

Note on the Text/Translation

Alain Badiou's *Métaphysique du bonheur réel* was first published in the series *Métaphysique S*, edited by Élie During, Patrice Maniglier, Quentin Meillassoux and David Rabouin for Presses Universitaires de France in 2015. This translation — of which more in the translators' Introduction — was done over the course of 2015. *Happiness*, the book's current English title, a radical truncation of the full title *Metaphysics of Real Happiness*, was mandated by publishing concerns. Reasons for Badiou's original choice of title are discussed in the Introductions below.

Translators' Foreword: Happiness Is Revolting

A.J. Bartlett and Justin Clemens

A matter of form

The last thing that the work of Alain Badiou can be said to be lacking is the means to speak in its own terms or, as he insists, 'in its own name.' The present text is no exception. As has often been said, Badiou is his own best exegete. So why another introduction? Despite the threat of superfluity, the demand for further exegesis is built into what Badiou conceptualises. The invention of concepts is for Badiou always also an invention of a new form, both the form of its possible consistency and the means of its transmission, in the manner aspired to by the French psychoanalyst Jacques Lacan of 'integral transmission.' In *Being and Event,* the formal means by which being is inscribed is paramount; in *Logics of Worlds*, that by which being *appears* is renovated; and, in the forthcoming *Immanence of Truths*, the question concerns the specificity of a truth in the form of a truth itself. Surely 'Happiness' too deserves a short detour through the means, which is to say the metaphysics, of its real form.

In Badiou's three 'big books' mathematical formalisation — set theory, category theory, and paraconsistent logic — is presented as integral to thought, as what can *be* thought. Here we encounter the thought of what there is, of what it is possible for thought to think of what there is, and the form by which what there is can come to be. Built into this mathematical formalisation is the injunction to think that which is *not* being qua being and whose existence is in exception to both being as such and the law of a world. The mathematical condition, as Badiou philosophically explains it, is the form of being and of being appearing that can be thought which includes within its exposition — consistent with it, integral to it — the very possibility of that which it is not. For Badiou, the task of a philosophy dedicated to the event is to think this *as* exception, whose *site* ontology provides, *as philosophy*, to invent philosophy under the formal conditions of its time. Set theory, for Badiou, writes being. Its writing is being's formalisation. Logic, the 'greater logic' of category theory, writes *being there*. What it is for what is — thus elemental being — is 'to be' or *exist* with others. Category theory is, *for* philosophy, an immanent theory of being with others, of relations, purely and simply. In the imminent third book, *Immanence of Truths*, the new formalism introduced 'on a large scale is paraconsistent negation, which explicitly contradicts the principle of non-contradiction. This formalism allows, when considering a truth, for contradictory perceptions to co-exist without interrupting the unity of this truth.' Three forms, three concepts: the generic, association, interiority.

What is most profoundly at stake, what concerns the fundamental 'turning of the world upside down,' to paraphrase Callicles' accusation against Socrates — a turning that makes us all decidedly anxious, the great dissembler warns — is that the onto-logy of Badiou's texts is fundamentally new. It is a new and newly possible treatment of an integral and insistent philosophical treatment. What set theory formalises, what category theory and paraconsistency formalise in turn — which is to say, what insists as true of these forms of thought — is that the One is not. Fundamentally, Georg Cantor's discovery of denumerable and uncountable infinites or the impossibility of the infinite being One and thus the conceptual impossibility of it being marked as the place of some One, God, Nature or History (or Market) and thereby operative as potential or virtual or ineffable, means that philosophy, under such a condition, must be the rethinking of all that pertains to it from the point of view of this 'actual' infinite. If the One is not, everything and every relation must be rethought. Badiou's classical philosophical categories of being, appearing, truth, subject, which he maintains against the temper of the times, which sees in ineffable multiplicity their final and finite deposition, are essentially new words in philosophy. Badiou's deployment of them is not a return to classicism, but the means of an entirely new formalisation of what these names present to thought. Philosophy, which is always *a* philosophy, recommences on new foundations: those given to it by the new discoveries in the thought of its time.

That there are mathematical 'infinite infinities' changes what philosophy has thought since Aristotle. Badiou is perhaps the only philosopher to take this absolute change in the relation between the finite and the infinite (thus undermining the relations of one and many, whole and parts) seriously, rationally, and thus to render its formal consequences. As a result, any philosophy which still orients itself in the final instance to the 'old' infinite of essence, potential, virtual, or some One is, by definition, not only out of date but inconsistent. At least, that is, if you credit mathematics with the power to think consistency as such; which is to say, with rationality; which is to say, with thinking rationally the inconsistency of being as such. If you don't credit that mathematics is a thought, then all bets are off and anything goes. But then you would be mistaken in thinking that this situation ensured infinite creativity or the free play of identities or difference. Rather, such a refusal is equivalent to accepting an ontology of the most extensive conformity and the most docile consensus.

Yet form is not the province of mathematics alone. For mathematics is the onto-logy of which philosophy treats: there is also to be invented or to be written in philosophy the form of politics, of art and of love. Badiou famously names these four disciplines mathematics, politics, art and love the 'conditions of philosophy.' As he unequivocally states in this book: 'there are not only the formalisms: in fact, they are only a sort of scaffolding for the conceptual construction and they assume a good dose of intuition.' For Badiou, these conditions *think* — they are the form of what they create and construct, just as a set is only the elements that make it up. What is at stake in these conditions is an 'invariance' in terms of event, address, praxis and consequence. Their form, whose existence is this invariance, is integral to the truth of these conditions insofar as this invariance insists in any world, under any logic, within any representation of these conditions relative to a world.

These conditions — mathematics, art, politics and love — present invariantly in every world in which they are variably represented. This invariability, beyond or despite or perhaps as immanent to its re-presentation, must be given its form and thus must be thought, and to think this invariability as what is true of these conditions, as in themselves truth procedures, is what philosophy does. Philosophy is the formalisation of a truth or the formalisation of the truths of its time. Ontology may be the being of any truth, but Badiou insists there is no truth of being: only its rational inscription, its form. As he notes in the *Metaphysics of Real Happiness*, there are three parts to this claim: 'truth from the point of view of its being; truth from the point of view of its worldly relations; and, to come, truth from the point of view of the interiority of the procedure of its own becoming.' This is the triple task of Badiou's 'big books.'

Small books and their schema: introjective/projective

If such formalisation is the project of Badiou's big books, let's consider the case of the 'small books' he writes in between those treatises that define, consolidate and specify his philosophical oeuvre — on the basis of which this century will no doubt ultimately become 'Badiouean.' What *are* the short works, what is *this* short work? Why does he write such small books at all?

Like all questions, this divides into two. There are certain small books that make obvious sense. Clearly, the first and second *Manifestos for Philosophy* need no justification even if their form as manifestos is deliberately striking and unreconciled. Then there are texts such as *Metapolitics*, the brilliantly named *Short Course on Transitory Ontology*, *Handbook Of Inaesthetics*, *The Meaning of Sarkozy*, *The Rebirth of History* and so on, each serving to illuminate the immanence of an invariance or a truth to *its* condition and the effective consequences of this truth within these discourses themselves. Or, more specifically in the cases of *The Meaning of Sarkozy* and *The Rebirth of History* and also of *The Century*, Badiou intervenes into how our present presents itself — as reaction, as riot, as real — according to the integral form offered up by the philosophical present established in the big books.

Leaving aside an account of what each of the small books specifically does, relative to the big books we can say they each have two invariant functions: introjective and projective. If we uncouple the first term from its more familiar psychoanalytical sense, the small books are an instance of internalising, enacting, extending and transmitting what is formalised by the big books. Hence in *Saint Paul: The Foundation of Universalism,* there is a subjectification of the formal theory of the subject of *Being and Event*; similarly, in *The Rebirth of History*, we find an analysis of the notion that 'it is right to rebel,' that rebellion is its own reason, that in the act is its idea, elucidated in the terms of the threefold schema of change formalised in *Logics of Worlds*.

Again, let's insist that this is not what purist empiricists, pious relativists, or sophisticated democrats sneer at as philosophy imposing itself as ideal on matter, but simply a thinking of what there is in 'matter' of its form: what it is and appears to be, the manner of its manifestation and the consequences for thought to which it gives rise. If, as Plato's Parmenides noted, this minimum of form cannot be granted to thought, to what it is to think, then we can have no discourse: that is, nothing to share. Hence, these short books are an act of thought and of a thought for which things and not words provide the impetus. Or a thought consecrated to the act as such, thus, following Marx's challenge, to real change. The thinking of true change, which is the form of real change, is, as Badiou notes, the force of all his work. So this is the introjective aspect.

The projective aspect (happily, 'projection' is a category of both geometry and analysis), which, as we see, touches on the introjective as its other side, is the putting into the world of the form of thought as its own act. Moreover, as acts of thought these small books carry a mode of seizure in the very form of their transmission as active thought. The form is transferred to the act — is transferential — and the subject will be constituted as he or she, anyone at all being equally disposed to think, who, seized in the act, pursues the form. A critical aspect of this seizure, whose essence is the transference — thus love! — is clearly decision. So seized the subject is that which decides to go on with 'being seized'.

Clearly, if it's a decision one can take the point or leave it. But curiously, there is in the reception of Badiou — let's use this passive term for a passive affect — a symptom. Like Plato, especially, but also Hegel and even Marx, Badiou has started to appear in texts and in talks by 'philosophers' as a figure whose dismissal must be announced. It is now not enough to ignore his work, which is fair and decisive enough, one must pronounce on it in public as that which must not be pronounced. This is itself a symptom of seizure, which need not at all lead into the sort of participation we are suggesting is consequentially decisive. In such cases, no participation is evident; indeed, it is proscribed.

Sophistry is by definition the occlusion of participation — of a participation in truth, of finding out (for yourself) its possible form. And thus sophistry, old and new, is a pedagogy of always sliding back into the security of what is, the conformities on offer, the better to continue to make one's way in some measure of relative comfort. It is not that Badiou is or presents *the* truth, but that Badiou qua philosopher in participating decisively, formally, actively, in its pursuit opens it up (again) to participation: to transference, transmission, consequence, *subject*. Badiou marks yet again, as all philosophy is wont to do, what is in exception to opinion, consensus, or, as he presciently noted in *Theory of the Subject*, 'the *pedagogy* of the world as it goes' (emphasis added).[1] The short books punctuate our times — what Badiou calls the times of 'restoration' — with their

---

[1] A. Badiou, *Theory of the Subject*, trans. with intro. B. Bosteels (London: Continuum, 2009), p. 302. Trans. mod.

exception, their education, and as such, for sophistry, what is there truly must be made to not be.

This double of introjection and projection is invariant in all Badiou's small books. Yet, precisely given this nature, we must not underestimate their specificity. Indeed, there are a couple of anomalous texts in this sequence: this one, *Happiness*, and *Ethics: An Essay on the Understanding of Evil*. We say 'anomalous' because, unlike the concepts broached and justified in the grand treatises and put to work in the little intermediary books, Badiou nowhere else talks about ethics or happiness as integral to philosophy. These two small books are therefore something like a negative version of what we have described: an ethics against Ethics, the Ethics of philosophy courses, of moral philosophy after (but not really *after*) Aristotle, and a happiness against the happiness of this same moral philosophy and most especially against its puerile avatars (the only description possible) in all forms of psychology. This, as we will further explain below, is merely the consensual and phony empiricism providing the increasingly necessary soul supplement of the dominant material forces.

Of course, these topics clearly pertain to the history of philosophy. But for Badiou, finally, insofar as they are a matter for philosophy, philosophically rendered in the way they are after Aristotle — which is to say also after Plato as read through Aristotle (as so much scholarship still does)[2] and

---

[2] Debra Nails makes the point that many contemporary 'Platonists' read Plato through Aristotelian eyes. See *Agora, Academy, and the Conduct of Philosophy* (Dordrecht: Kluwer Academic, 1995), p. 224. In the notes to *Logics of Worlds*, Badiou asserts that all contemporary anti-Platonists, those 'doctrinaires of sense' who oppose 'mathematisation', be they hermeneuticists or sophists, are all, at base

without recourse to a formalisation irreducible to discourses of some One or of 'opinion' — philosophy stands as obstacle. In other words, their representation in philosophy and in the discourses of these philosophies' avatars — in *Ethics* we see this in discourses of the other, identity and 'Human Rights' — is an act of the impossibility of an 'ethics of truths' (the only kind for Badiou) or, as in the present book, 'true happiness.' It is impossible within these moral philosophies of ethics or happiness to think of ethics or happiness. This is because, as Badiou says in his first *Manifesto for Philosophy*, paraphrasing Saint Just, whom he quotes more than once in the present text, 'truth is a new word in Europe (and elsewhere too).'[3]

Truth is a new word in two ways. First, even if moral philosophy invokes a notion of truth, it is rendered atavistic and inconsistent by the new theory of the infinite; second, truth is obfuscated in the discourses of the linguistic turn (such as deconstruction, phenomenology, analytic philosophy, vitalism), each of which by different routes gives contemporary opinion its currency. Badiou's formal theory of truth demands that the thought of ethics and of happiness is not *opposed* to these contemporary representations but *subtracted* from them. 'To be thought' at all, ethics and happiness require an *other* orientation to the present itself. Hence we can see the book on *Ethics* as an

---

'Aristotelians'. *Logics of Worlds*, trans. Alberto Toscano (London: Continuum, 2009), p. 548.

[3] Let's note that Saint Just says that 'happiness is a new word in Europe' in order to emphasise that it signifies a happiness nowhere visible, despite the fact that the word is used constantly by the *ancien regime*. True happiness exceeds its representation.

intervention. An intervention on a consensus — which is already a negative one — that there is no truth regarding the ethical. If, as noted, this consensus is arrived at in different ways, it remains *the* shared fundamental orientation. Beneath the constant ethical squabbling and prevarications, *there is* a consensus. As Badiou says in the essay 'A Speculative Disquisition on the Concept of Democracy' in *Metapolitcs:* 'Since Plato, philosophy has stood for a rupture with opinion, and is meant to examine everything that is spontaneously considered as normal....the philosopher demands that we examine the norm of this normality.'[4] An integral aspect of philosophical work is the reconstruction of the underlying logics of the present in terms that they themselves must dissimulate and disavow.

This brings us to happiness. It is clear to see that it has suffered a similar fate to ethics. It has fallen to the psychologists to define and categorise it for us, to establish it as predicate for the vapid subjectivity the contemporary world prescribes as norm. Not coincidentally, 'happiness' is also a shibboleth for the good democrats of parliamentary-capitalism, for whom it equates with security and the enjoyment and service of goods. This non-coincident consensus: psychology, providing the debilitating pseudoscience of the adaptable, flexible, resilient subject; and parliamentary capitalism, proving the force of its law as its only good. Both, educated by philosophies *without* truth, have come to exhaust or, better, occlude all thought in the matter. It is no wonder that anxiety is targeted for eradication in

---

[4] A. Badiou, *Metapolitics*, trans. Jason Barker (London: Verso, 2005), p. 79.

our states striving for satisfaction, for if, as Lacan says, 'it doesn't lie,' anxiety is *the* symptom capable of pointing out the horror of the consensual prison house of every subject.[5] Anxiety must be ruled out or at least localised in the psyches of maladapted individuals, those somehow resistant to consumption, the better to protect the structure of this 'best of all possible worlds' from any questions as to its lack. Any subjectivity not in thrall to its satisfaction is questionable, which is at the same time the satisfaction of the state. So, as regards 'happiness,' the protocols are set: localise the anxiety in the individual by presupposing a theory of self already divorced from structure, which gets structure off the hook; attack the individual, adjusting and expanding the ego's 'distortions' and 'maladaptions' through the incursions of cognitive 'homework,' thereby having it normed by the structure; finally, affirm that the resultant enforced consent is the only true satisfaction. Anxiety is thus curbed and cured in an abusive instance of the *pharmakon*. Happiness ensues — if not for the patient, at least for the purveyors of happiness — as the name of a consensus in the way of the world.

So Badiou writes this small book, *The Metaphysics of Real Happiness*, with the same intent as that of *Ethics*: that there must be true happiness other than as this ordinary, consensual or representational form today named 'satisfaction.' 'All philosophy,' he announces here, 'even and above all when it is buttressed by complex scientific knowledges, innovative works

---

[5] See J. Lacan, *Anxiety: The Seminar of Jacques Lacan, Book X*, ed. J.-A. Miller (Cambridge: Polity, 2014).

of art, revolutionary politics, intense loves — is a metaphysics of happiness, or it's not worth an hour of trouble.' This way, in both anxious *and* courageous revolt, happiness lies.

The happy desire of metaphysics

In this philosophical return to happiness against its capture by the partisans of normalization, Badiou is also necessarily returning to the history of philosophy itself. If happiness is perhaps one of the most basic and universal of human goals, it is also one of the greatest themes of ancient philosophy. *What is happiness?* and *What do I have to do to be happy?* are its fundamental questions. Yet part of the difficulty of happiness is that answers of the type 'Never eat beans' or 'Watch two hours of television maximum a day' are probably not going to cut it for very long, no matter how adaptive to reality they purport to be. If it were simply a matter of following a strict regimen or submitting oneself to the dictates of clear, distinct and well-delimited injunctions, then humans might be able to be happy in cults and totalitarian formations. This, however, does not always seem to be the case.

If not everybody is able to tolerate such solutions, it is because happiness is born from a certain obscurity or aporia. Moreover, it is not for the want of choice of different models of behaviour that happiness remains opaque. On the contrary: much of the dynamism and diversity of ancient philosophy is driven by a deep acknowledgement of the divisions and divergences of human being, from Persia to the Piraeus. One of the consequences of such an acknowledgement, as Leo Strauss once put it, is that the evidence of such empirical differences — if they are not accepted as a question of mere contingent variation in themselves — lead to an absolutely fundamental distinction, that between 'nature' and 'culture'. 'The distinction between nature and convention', Strauss writes, 'between *physis* and *nomos*, is therefore coeval with the discovery of nature and hence with philosophy'.[6] Philosophy as such begins with this rift. Even if philosophy may subsequently seek to reduce or exacerbate the claims of the distinction, it nonetheless requires both explanation and intervention if one is to meet the test of reason. In other words, the philosophical questions concerning happiness turn *simultaneously* on intimate experience and a divided social nature.

Yet the questions of happiness are thereby not only personal and social, but quite literally cosmological as well. If our own nature is not simply or unilaterally given, what is our relation to nature? What accounts for the patent indetermination or play between the circumstances of our birth and our possibilities for living? Should we return to a natural way that our culture has left or lost, or should we emphasize or exacerbate our own unnatural nature? It turns out that, for every significant ancient philosophical intervention, such questions demand the construction of radical and sophisticated forms of metaphysics

---

[6] L. Strauss, *Natural Right and History* (Chicago and London: The University of Chicago Press, 1965), p. 90.

as an essential part of the answer. If there is no question more physical, personal and pressing than that of happiness, it turns out that no possible answer can circumvent the chicanes of metaphysics.

From the simplicity of the question to the complexity of the response, happiness quickly becomes a violently polemical affair. For Plato, happiness is conditional upon justice, that is, upon the proper structuring of the city itself. The affects delivered by unconstrained Eros are tyrannical; they must be curbed by the claims of knowledge. In response, Aristotle famously speaks of *eudaemonia* and the highest good, to be achieved through the active practice of virtue in accordance with reason. For the Stoics, by contrast, happiness derives from acting in accordance with necessity, the unbreakable laws of the cosmos, accompanied by a kind of affect of indifference. The Epicureans, abominating both Plato and the Stoics, considered that life must lived according to a mode that seeks pleasure and avoids pain, and whose emblem is withdrawal from the political world to a garden with friends.

What is perhaps most misleading about such crude dictionary-type summaries is their circumvention of the logic of presentation, argumentation, and justification crucial to these philosophies — including their often-outrageous cosmic visions. The fine details of the relations that each philosophy forges between pleasure and pain, between law and duty, necessity and contingency, knowledge and opinion, convention and nature are almost entirely lost. These details concern the problem of affect, and thus that of body and embodiment; of modality, and therefore the problematic of encounters and events; of epistemology, and as a consequence the ways and implications of our knowing (and not-knowing); of ontology, and thereby the status of existences beyond our own. Tedious as such argumentation is often held to be, for philosophers, true happiness can only be found in precisely going through such metaphysical demonstrations. Their fierce disputes also share something that remains intensely at stake for Badiou in the present book: true happiness requires philosophy. Moreover — and this is perhaps even more surprising — a philosopher's life is the happiest life of all.

As we have already indicated, such convictions are rare in the contemporary world. They can appear unjustifiable, even provocatively risible. I went to the Academy, one might think, and all I got there was this lousy metaphysics! Yet such a reaction hardly prevents questions of happiness from remaining as insistent and intractable as ever. This is not least because, as the aforementioned Saint-Just notoriously announced, happiness became a directly political question in European modernity. There is no more famous nor influential instance than the *United States Declaration of Independence*, which reads: 'We hold these truths to be self-evident, that all men are created equal, that they are endowed by their Creator with certain unalienable Rights, that among these are Life, Liberty and the pursuit of Happiness.' With revolutionary modernity, happiness becomes a right for which the state itself is the guarantor. With the coeval and mutually-conditioning rights of life and liberty, happiness is now the goad, the goal, and the ground for all meaningful action. As Lacan acerbically remarks, this attitude implicitly destroys the very basis of Aristotle's Sovereign Good. In its place, we find the hedonistic calculus of Benthamite utilitarianism and, as Lacan adds, a new sanctification of the bureaucrat, who — as at once limit and operator of the new social access to our desire for happiness — becomes the very model of the modern saint, seeking to promote the goods of and for all.[7]

Yet it is possible that happiness has recently and decisively entered a post-political phase. No longer a topic for revolutionary committees, happiness is now a feature of health and productivity commissions, corporate well-being programs, and psychopharmacological experimentation. If it remains at the centre of political calculations, particularly in our so-called democratic nations where modulating the opinions and affects of voters are integrally at stake, this must be at the cost of its commodification. Happiness has to come at a price — and for something to hold its price in the world-market, it must be constantly disrupted, repackaged, and redistributed, in a relentless slew of research, development, intervention, and retraction.

Yet if happiness is now a commodity, it is one of those commodities — like energy products — which help to keep making other commodities. Unhappy workers don't work as hard, they get uppity or sick or die, they cost time and money. Moreover, since everybody allegedly spontaneously seeks

---

[7] See J. Lacan, *The Ethics of Psychoanalysis (1959–1960)*, trans. D. Porter (London: Routledge, 1992).

happiness — or at least ought to do so — the theme becomes a privileged means and justification for further incursions of the security state and corporate governance routines. As a result, as William Davies has recently enumerated in *The Happiness Industry*, global corporations now seek 'wisdom' from Tibetan monks and Big Pharma, at the same time that they pitilessly extend their reach into physiology and psychology, inverting even doctors' 'sick notes' into 'fit notes,' or reconceiving personal leisure choices, such as going for a walk, as aids to productivity.[8] Happiness is precisely not encouraged or sought for itself, but only to enhance the flexibility, productivity and consumption-power of populations.

We are even witnesses to new kinds of Pythagoreanism, whereby happiness becomes the privileged object of cults of cognitive rationality. As Jennifer Kahn recently reported for *The New York Times Magazine*: 'Our minds, cobbled together over millenniums by that lazy craftsman, evolution, are riddled with bad mental habits.... These "cognitive errors" ripple through our lives, CFAR [the Center for Applied Rationality] argues, and underpin much of our modern malaise.'[9] Note some of the key presumptions here: 'reason' is identified almost entirely

---

[8] See W. Davies, *The Happiness Industry* (London: Verso, 2015). It might even be worth asking what lessons contemporary capital has drawn from the failures of the great communist states of the twentieth century, including the ideas of Trotskyist 'permanent revolution' parleyed into managerial 'continuing disruption' and 'disruptive marketing,' or the Maoist cultural revolutionaries as cadres of well-disciplined shock troops aggressively calling out evidence of ideological transgressions — a kind of corporate goon squad of happiness.

[9] J. Kahn, 'The Happiness Code,' *The New York Times Magazine*, 14 January 2016,

with 'cognition' of an instrumental or technical kind; the 'good' that is 'happiness' is equivalent to individual self-optimization; such self-optimization demands the ongoing escalation of technical monitoring of the body itself, right down into previously-inaccessible molecular recesses. In maximizing the productivity and exploitability of human resources, happiness is a key corporate provision. We have come a long way from the search of the ancients for the secret of happiness — not least by ratcheting up the desire for rational control of the body to unprecedented levels.

For such reasons, it might seem tempting to repudiate the discourse of happiness altogether, as irremediably corrupt. In fact, this has been the strategy of an ongoing line of critique of which psychoanalysis was one of the major twentieth-century proselytizers. As Sigmund Freud very famously announced in 1893:

When I have promised my patients help or improvement by means of a cathartic treatment I have often been faced by this objection: Why, you tell me yourself that my illness is probably connected with my circumstances and the events of my life. You cannot alter these in any way. How do you propose to help me, then?' And I have been able to make this reply: 'No doubt fate would find it easier than I do to relieve you of your illness. But you will be able to convince yourself

http://www.nytimes.com/2016/01/17/magazine/the-happiness-code.html?_r=0
Accessed 23 February 2016.

that much will be gained if we succeed in transforming your hysterical misery into common unhappiness. With a mental life that has been restored to health you will be better armed against that unhappiness.'[10]

Note that Freud's ambitions are already not those of a straight-forward 'cure,' as if a psychiatrist or psychologist was ever in the position of being able to provide such a thing. Freud is quite clear that, if happiness is indeed an ideal, it is not something that he can provide. Rather, he can help a patient to come to what he calls 'common unhappiness,' that is, to become somebody at the mercy more of their external circumstances than of their own neurotic pain. Unlike many contemporary psychologies — many of which are in fact Freud's inheritors in one or another respect — Freud never forgot the role that social immiseration played in the constitution of action.

But society can't be blamed for everything! As psychoanalysis developed over the course of the next decades, Freud elaborated a position in which happiness is essentially impossible, and in which our fantasies of happiness are integral to our unhap-piness. Happiness is impossible because the agency that might register such a thing — the ego itself — is beset on all sides by its own conditions of existence, its irremediable dependence on forces that are irreducibly exogenous and endogenous. As Freud

---

[10] S. Freud, 'The Psychotherapy of Hysteria' from J. Breuer and S. Freud, *Studies on Hysteria* in *The Standard Edition of the Complete Psychological Works of Sigmund Freud, Vol. II (1893–1895)*, ed. J. Strachey (London: The Hogarth Press and the Institute of Psycho-Analysis), p. 305.

writes in *The Ego and the Id* (1923), 'we see this same ego as a poor creature owing service to three masters and consequently menaced by three dangers: from the external world, from the libido of the id, and from the severity of the super-ego.'[11] As such, the *forcing* of happiness by external agencies — whatever its motivations and means — constitutes yet another assault on the subject, one that can moreover make a happy compact with the internal persecutory agency of the super-ego.

One could then suggest that contemporary cognitive accounts of 'negative emotions' thereby err not only in applying such a scale as 'positive' and 'negative' to the field of emotions at all, but also actively contribute to making happiness impossible. Such an outcome would not only be evident at the scale of population studies in the forms of rates of suicide or of so-called 'epidemics' of anxiety and depressive disorders ('stress,' 'burn-out,' 'career crisis') but, pragmatically and locally, in the fact that the alibi of happiness is used to license and extend the aggressiveness of demands upon the ego itself. It is partially for such reasons that Lacan notes that there is something tragic — in the full sense of the word — about happiness for humanity, and invokes Sophocles' *Antigone* as the place where a demand for happiness encounters its limit in a 'criminal good.' As he puts it, citing the Greek: 'It's odd that in almost all languages happiness

---

[11] S. Freud, *The Ego and the Id* in *The Standard Edition of the Complete Psychological Works of Sigmund Freud, Volume XIX (1923–1925)*, ed. J. Strachey (London: The Hogarth Press and the Institute of Psycho-Analysis, 1961), p. 56.

offers itself in terms of a meeting — *tuché*.[12] The etymology of happiness returns it to an event or an encounter, to the province of Chance, the return of the real against the automata of habit and sociability.

But where does this leave us? We have sketched out a kind of fundamental antagonism at the heart of happiness today. On the one hand, we are subject to the tyranny of a happiness corrupted by a managerialism which, as Plato says in the *Theatetus*, boasts of how much milk it is able to squeeze from its herds. Happiness is promoted by the most iniquitous of capitalist instrumentalities. On the other hand, the strongest intellectual critiques of happiness suggest that, as practice, concept and ideal, happiness has an irreducible bond to persecution, criminality, and death and that it is, in the end, impossible.

Philosophy Established Between the Intolerable and the Impossible

It is in the light of this irreducible antagonism between the intolerable and the impossible that we are able to see something extraordinary about Badiou's philosophical method as such. In this book, Badiou expressly confronts, first, the corporate partisans of happiness on their own terrain, and, second, the strong critiques of happiness coming from a psychoanalytic provenance, what Badiou would call

---

[12] Lacan, *Ethics*, p. 13.

an *anti*-philosophical source. Here, Badiou does precisely what he claims a philosopher ought to do. On the one hand, the present corruption of happiness by state psychology is nonetheless pointing to something real that has been corrupted, something that, even in its corruption, is calling for its own liberation. That element must be liberated. On the other hand, the very real critique of happiness by antiphilosophy offers a challenge to every philosopher: to meet that challenge at its strongest point and overthrow it. A new idea of happiness must be constructed. *To redeem the real from its present corruption by binding it to an idea that confronts the challenge of the strongest critique of that idea* — this is one of the fundamental tasks for philosophy.

But there is more. Here, this perennial injunction of philosophy is further complicated by the fact that it forces Badiou to change his own previously tenaciously held positions. What is unexpected is Badiou's desire to introduce a *properly philosophical affect*: happiness itself! Previously, Badiou had at most underlined the *indifference* of philosophy in its seizing of the affects attendant upon the generic procedures. As he writes in *Conditions*, the task of philosophy is to:

— Envisage love solely according to the truth that hatches on the Two of sexuation, and on the Two tout court. But without the tension of pleasure-displeasure kept in play by the love-object.

— Envisage politics as truth of the infinite of collective situations, as a treatment in truth of this infinite, but without the enthusiasm or sublimity of these situations themselves.

— Envisage mathematics as a truth of multiple-being in and through the letter, as a power of literalization, but without the intellectual beatitude of the resolved problem.

— And last envisage the poem as a truth of sensible presence lodged in rhythm and image but without the corporeal captation of rhythm and image.[13]

The reader will note that, if certain intense affects are expressly identified with particular conditions, Badiou is careful to detach philosophy from any one of these affects. The key phrase here is that philosophy, in relation to the affects of its conditions, is 'but without.' Indeed, philosophy as a thinking of the thinking of its conditions not only cannot be reduced to any particular affect or set of affects, but is even potentially *other* to all affect. In this regard, the only 'affect' specific to philosophy would be a paradoxical one, denominated by a host of ancient philosophies under variable headings of 'indifference' (e.g., *ataraxia, apatheia, adiaphora*).

This is because Badiou's metaphysics from *Being and Event* onwards has established and insisted upon a stringent difference between 'truths,' the work of the four conditions that are science, art, love and politics' and 'Truth,' the idea generated by philosophy itself to ensure that the divergent truths of its own time are

---

[13] A. Badiou, *Conditions*, trans. S. Corcoran (London: Continuum, 2008), p. 44.

nonetheless all 'compatible' or 'compossible.' For Badiou, one can only be a subject if a truth is in play. Philosophy deals with Truth, not truth: there is therefore no subject of philosophy; there is therefore no affect proper to philosophy; if a name must be given to the non-affect of philosophy, it is indifference.

We must underline that 'affect' for Badiou is not simply a sensation or a feeling or an emotion, but an effect of subjective experimental reasoning in a particular genre. Partially this is due to Badiou's constitutional hostility to what he sees as the fundamental category of the value of life crucial to currently dominant forms of power, above all what he calls democratic materialism. As he remarks of Gilles Deleuze, 'most of his concepts were sucked up, so to speak, by the *doxa* of the body, desire, affect, networks, the multitude, nomadism and enjoyment into which a whole contemporary "politics" sinks.'[14] 'Affect,' then, if it is itself to be redeemed from its present corruption, must be given a proper philosophical grounding. For Badiou in *Logics of Worlds*, 'it is indeed by its affect that the human animal recognizes that it participates, through its incorporated body, in some subject of truth.'[15] 'Affect' in this description is an effect: an effect-of-truth that confirms to the subject of that truth that truth is indeed at stake. This, it need hardly be said, is a highly rigorous and restricted conception of affect.

If the fundamental structure of this argumentation has been set for decades, Badiou has nonetheless occasionally changed

---

[14] Badiou, *Logics of Worlds*, p. 35.
[15] Badiou, *Logics of Worlds*, p. 480.

the names and distributions of his affects since *Theory of the Subject*, where he offers the diagrammatic quadrangle of 'anxiety,' 'courage,' 'superego,' and 'justice' (the reader will note that of this list only 'anxiety' is regularly counted in everyday exchange as something approximating an affect).[16] In *Logics of Worlds*, he provides the following identifications: politics, enthusiasm; arts, pleasure; love, happiness; science, joy. In the present book, the list has been altered slightly: the *joie* of science has here become *beatitude* (*béatitude*, derived from the Latin *beatitudo,* a concept of crucial importance to Spinoza); whereas the *plaisir* of love has become *joie*, joy.

This redistribution has had to take place because *happiness* is now needed for philosophy itself. As Badiou confesses in the present book, attending to happiness forces the acknowledgement that this may be the affect proper to philosophy or to the philosopher herself. If this maintains the very sharp distinction between (true) happiness and (mere animal) satisfaction familiar to students of philosophy and religion from ancient times to the present, it threatens the absolutely crucial identification between affect and truths, as well as the distinction between philosophy and its conditions.

Although this is one of Badiou's small books, and, in some ways, a modest one, let us underline in the most decisive fashion just how radical and surprising the implications of this redistribution are, especially for those who have followed Badiou's philosophical development over the last few decades. Not only does this book revivify the dialectic of introjection

---

[16] See Badiou, *Theory of the Subject*, *passim*, e.g., p. 303.

and projection familiar from his previous small books; not only does it exemplify the philosophical work of the defence and reconstruction of a concept between the intolerable and the impossible; but it announces an imminent transformation of an absolutely key element of Badiou's philosophy. The philosopher is not only happy, he or she alone knows true happiness. We will have to wait for the final volume in Badiou's great philosophical trilogy — the long-awaited *Immanence of Truths* — to see the full metaphysical justification of this claim.

Translating Happiness

It is *de rigueur* in prefaces to translated texts to bemoan the translator's task. We do not recoil from these liturgical exigencies here. It is also standard to discuss words and concepts that proved particularly problematic; again, we will shortly give some instances of these. Yet, in remarking the difficulty of the translator's enterprise as a whole, plus the idiomatic and personal vicissitudes of keywords and key-expressions, we would also like to mark what we have been able to learn about Badiou's thought more generally — including the form of its presentation — from this particular book.

First of all, as discussed above, it has confirmed that there is a kind of relation between the big and small books of Badiou's. Not only do the little books reiterate and put to work concepts established and justified in the big ones, but these little books embody a kind of introjective-projective dialectic of the concept. Yet there is more. The little books are certainly popularizing in straightforward ways: short and accessibly-written, they also take place somewhere between speech and writing, understood in an everyday sense. Not only have they been delivered and re-forged over a long period as lectures in a number of languages, all over the world, but, over time, what began as independent strands of thought in Badiou himself come to be re-worked into a single text, united by a concept which has perhaps only belatedly emerged from what was already there.

This of course is a standard 'feedback' principle familiar to educators from time immemorial: in the diversity and heat of presentation and discussion, previously unthematised or obscure concepts can emerge, be clarified, consolidated, and extended. Plato's *Dialogues* are one preeminent *locus classicus* in which this procedure is both staged and embodied as such, and in which the character-event Socrates proves a privileged locus of pedagogical polemic. If Badiou certainly retains Plato as a model in some fundamental aspects of his work, this is not always the case. Insofar as the little books are *re*-presentations of Badiou's thought that has been worked out in the big books, then the former become more reliant upon the natural language for their effects. Most of the small books are accordingly lacking the minatory formalisations (the technical *writing*) essential to the larger treatises. As a result, Badiou not only has recourse to idiomatic French phrases, but begins to rely on the free variation of certain shorthand circumlocutions to relay his own well-founded formal motifs. To give several brief examples: we find him speaking of 'truth-procedures' as well as 'protocols of truth,' or, alternatively, 'movements,' 'trends,' and 'orientations.'

In one sense, these are merely stylistic modulations deriving from a kind of spontaneous rhetoric of delivery, familiar from all kinds of public presentation. No fundamental conceptual differences depend on them. Yet their very variability is also paradoxically tied to a kind of *logical pedagogy*. If it is important — as Badiou himself reminds us in this book — to avoid the deadening hand of academicism, it is also important to mark the fact that Badiou is articulating his declarations with serious arguments (which cannot always be given their amplitude in the smaller books). One of the problems for this translation was therefore to try to emphasize the transmission of thought by way of both rhetorical accessibility *and* logical structure. For instance, as Lia Hills has reminded us, Badiou's use of the word 'movement' might remind us of the architectonics of a musical piece.

In a large sense, the difference between spoken and written English is different from the difference between spoken and written French. Hypotactical markers in English — thus, therefore, thereby, moreover, however, etc. — can often themselves come across as otiose or academic, slowing down while adding nothing to the sense and reference of an argument. Nonetheless, we have insisted on keeping these, for a very specific reason: Badiou's work is utterly formal (logical, mathematical) all the way down. What might in other authors be mere tics or implicit forms of adherence to, say, a particular hierarchy of address, needs to be given its full demonstrative force.

At times, our own (over)identification with a certain ideal of rigour in Badiou's work could induce us to misrecognize idiomatic or common terms as technical ones. Whereas there is no question that *subjectivation* is a *terminus technicus* which has a variety of possible translations (sometimes given in English as 'subjectivization,' sometimes 'subjectivisation,' sometimes 'subjectivation,' sometimes 'subjectification,' etc.[17]), deriving from Lacan and repurposed by Badiou, how to translate '*à l'interieur*'? 'From the inside'? 'Within'? Does it designate a key innovation in the relation between a truth and its outsides? Probably not. It turns out that our perplexities were occasionally the *fata morgana* of our own technical gaze. As for the notorious *appareil* and *dispositif*, these may be extremely difficult terms to translate in Michel Foucault, Gilles Deleuze, and Giorgio Agamben, but it seems to us Badiou uses them in a far freer fashion: we have gone for the basic *apparatus* as a result. Regarding the word '*sens,*' which is everywhere in this text, we simply gave up. Instead of sometimes translating this as 'meaning,' we transliterated it throughout as *sense*. In the end, what is determining for Badiou is that philosophy must exceed whatever natural language it is written in. Unlike Heidegger, for whom Greek and German were the only languages of Being, for Badiou philosophy must be eminently translatable across languages.

Yet, at the level of the sentence and paragraph, Badiou can still maintain an extraordinary density of allusion. He very often

---

[17] In his translation of Lacan's *Ecrits*, Bruce Fink gives the note for *subjectivation*: 'The French here means either subjectification — turning someone (or something) into a subject — or the fact of rendering something subjective, which I have translated here as "subjectivization." Similarly, subjectiver (the verb form) can mean either to subjectify or to subjectivize. It is often unclear which term should be used,' *Ecrits* (New York: Norton, 2006), p. 765. Bosteels follows Fink in his translation of *Theory of the Subject*, whereas Alberto Toscano opts for 'subjectivation' in *Logics of Worlds*.

draws upon the vocabularies of otherwise unnamed interlocutors in local situations. For instance, one will find paragraphs that, although not explicitly concerned with Lacan in their content or argumentation, deploy the Lacanian vocabulary of demand, desire and drive. At other times, one can discern allusions to Jacques Rancière and his *le partage du sensible*, to Deleuze, to Marx, and many others. Words *in situ* can often allude to an unmarked figure or phrase whose thought has quietly licensed or has some bearing upon the claims propositionally expressed, e.g., '*entraves*', 'fetters', 'chains', should perhaps make us think of Rousseau's *Social Contract* and the *Communist Manifesto*, and so on. This allusiveness is undoubtedly also connected to a certain confidence in citation. As befits the projective nature of his little books, Badiou does not always provide full scholarly references for his quotations: where these bear on texts and utterances not always widely accessible, we have tried to restitute these here.

Let us give one final example of Badiou's procedure that has implications not only for this translation, but for our understanding of his thinking more generally. The title alone of the first chapter of this book 'Philosophy and the Desire of Philosophy' (*Philosophie et désir de philosophie*) gave us a number of headaches. We first decided for 'the desire for philosophy,' which certainly sounds more natural in English. Yet it quickly became clear that Badiou was playing on both subjective and objective senses of the genitive. For if there is certainly an emphasis in that chapter upon the desire *for* philosophy as it is legible in the world, philosophy's desire is simultaneously in question: *what does philosophy want*? In answering this question,

Badiou has recourse to a trope of *prosopopeia* or anthropomor-phisation: philosophy as itself a being that desires. Aside from this functioning as yet another level of allusion to the history of philosophy — one might think of Boethius' *The Consolations of Philosophy*, in which Lady Philosophy is an active allegorical figure — here it enables Badiou to provide a rhetorical double to his logical dialectics of philosophical interpellation. In this case, philosophy is personified as a sick or dying character — or perhaps rather a hypochondriacal one. The question of the desire of philosophy is therefore not only a question of the 'of,' but of analysing, then breaking, à la Plato, with the very medical model (that of the 'health of the body') that provides one of the strongest struts of contemporary biopower, not least regarding the physics and psychology of happiness.

This is undoubtedly why, on the final page of another recent short book, *In Search of the Lost Real*, following a brilliant close-reading of a poem of Pier Paolo Pasolini, Badiou objects to the former's sadness: 'Yet today, despite the mourning that thought imposes upon us, we must be convinced that searching for what real there is in the real can be — is — a joyful passion.'[18] For Badiou, then, an affective subjective experiment with life has once more returned to the heart of philosophy. Happiness has again become philosophically revolutionary on three fronts: against its corruption, against its critique, and against philosophy itself. Happiness must be revolting — or it will not be.

---

18 A. Badiou, *À la recherche du reel perdu* (Fayard, 2015), p. 60.

Introduction:
The Metaphysics of
Real Happiness

It is surely paradoxical to give the title *The Metaphysics of Real Happiness* to a book that seems above all concerned with discerning the tasks of philosophy, and which even engages towards the end in a description of my personal projects insofar as they touch on philosophy. Yet a mere glance at my major books would show that my philosophy is undoubtedly constructed, like all others, on the basis of a number of apparently very disparate elements, even if one might note the active function of materials rarely associated with happiness, such as set theory, the theory of sheaves of sets over Heyting algebras, or large infinities. And also the French, Russian, Chinese revolutions, of Robespierre, Lenin or Mao, all and each marked with the infamous seal of the Terror. Moreover, I have recourse to numerous poems held to be more hermetic than pleasurable, for example, those by Mallarmé, Pessoa, Wallace Stevens or Paul Celan. Or I take true love as an example, regarding which moralists and prudent persons have always noted that the sufferings it provokes and the banal reports of its fragility render its vocation for happiness doubtful. Notwithstanding that certain of my principal masters, for example Descartes or Pascal, Hegel or Kierkegaard, can hardly pass – at least at a first reading – for jolly souls. One can hardly see the relation between all this and a quiet life, the abundance of little everyday satisfactions, interesting work, an appropriate salary, an iron constitution, a happy couple, memorable holidays, lovely friends, a well-appointed household, a comfortable car, a sweet and faithful domestic pet, trouble-free and charming children who are successful at school: in short, what we usually and universally understand as 'happiness'.

To justify this paradox, I could of course shelter behind masters usually held to be unquestionable, for example Plato and Spinoza.

The former, in his *Republic*, makes a long mathematical education and the constant exertion of dialectical logic an imperative condition for any access to truths. He then demonstrates that only those abandoning their obeisance to dominant opinions, and faithful only to truths in which their thought 'participates' (it is Plato's word), can arrive at happiness. Because the dialectic – for which mathematics is the obligatory prelude – is nothing other than the rational and logical movement of thought, and this movement can be qualified as 'meta-physics' in the original sense of the word (it goes beyond what is reducible to a scientific physics), the bond between mathematics, logic and happiness finds itself entirely founded by a metaphysical point of view, which ensures the coherence of this bond. What is more: if from mathematics to the dialectic and from the dialectic to happiness the consequence is good, we will call 'metaphysics' the complete thought of this consequence. And as happiness is the infallible sign of all access to truths, and therefore the real goal of a life worthy of this name, we can certainly say that the trajectory and its complete reflection comprise a metaphysics of happiness.

The second, in his *Ethics*, begins by affirming that, if there had been no mathematics, the human animal would have remained forever ignorant, which means there would have been no access to any 'adequate idea' (this is Spinoza's lexicon). But the immanent participation of the human intellect with an adequate idea can occur according to two regimes, which Spinoza names the 'second kind' and the 'third kind' of knowledge. The second kind proceeds by the arduous route of demonstrations, which requires logic, whereas the third kind proceeds by an 'intellectual intuition' which is like the concentration in a point of all the stages of an argument, the immediate grasp, in God himself – that is, in the Whole – of a truth that is moreover deducible. Spinoza calls 'virtue' (Plato would undoubtedly say 'justice') the state of a human subject who achieves the complete knowledge of an adequate idea, because he could gain access through the third kind of knowledge. Finally, happiness (Spinoza uses the Latin word '*beatitudo*', which is stronger) is nothing other than the exercise of true thought, that is to say virtue: 'Happiness is not the reward of virtue, but virtue itself.'[1] In other words, happiness

---

[1] See B. de Spinoza, *The Ethics*, trans. E. Curley (London: Penguin, 1996), Bk V, P42,

is the affect of the True, which would not have existed were it not for mathematics, and could not have been concentrated in an intuition if it had not first been demonstrated. Henceforth, mathematics and logic comprise with intellectual intuition what we can perfectly well call a metaphysics of happiness.

In sum, all philosophy – even and above all when it is supported by complex scientific knowledges, innovative works of art, revolutionary politics, intense loves – is a metaphysics of happiness, or it's not worth an hour of our trouble. For why impose on thought and life the formidable tests of demonstration, the general logic of thinking, the intelligence of formalisms, the attentive reading of recent poems, the risky engagement in mass rallies, love without guarantee, if it is not because all this is necessary for true life finally to exist – that which Rimbaud said is absent, and of which we maintain, we philosophers who repudiate all forms of scepticism, cynicism, relativism and the shallow irony of the non-dupes, that true life can never be totally absent? What follows provides in four movements my own version of this certainty.

I first proceed to a general determination of what the interest of philosophy can be today, if it is at least capable of responding to the demands of the age. In other words, I clarify the reasons for which a human subject can (in fact, must, but this is another matter) nourish in itself a singular desire, that I very simply call the desire of philosophy. By way of an analysis of contemporary

---

p. 180. The word *beatitudo* is translated by Curley as 'blessedness'; here, we have modified this to 'happiness' to keep in line with Badiou's terminology and remarks.

constraints, I show that the situation of philosophy is today a defensive one, and that there is a further reason to sustain its desire. In doing so, I sketch the reasons why this support is in relation with the possibility of a real happiness.

In a second movement, to clarify what induces us in the direction of such happiness and its relation with the desire of philosophy, I speak of antiphilosophy, illustrated by a whole constellation of brilliant writers such as Pascal, Rousseau, Kierkegaard, Nietzsche, Wittgenstein, Lacan. My thesis is that these antiphilosophers, generally sceptical in regard to the possibility of being at once in the true and in beatitude, inclined towards the idea of the great value of sacrifice (even useless sacrifice), are nonetheless necessary to us in order that our classicism should not become an academicism, which is the principal enemy of philosophy, and therefore of happiness: ennui is in effect the affect by which academic discourse is infallibly recognized. In effect, it is the great antiphilosophers who teach us that all that possesses a true value is earned; not by the course of ordinary usages and the adoption of dominant ideas, but by the effect, existentially experienced, of a rupture with the course of the world.

In the third chapter, I get to grips with the question that the modern type, just like the committed Marxist, always addresses to the philosopher: 'What use are you, with your abstract ratiocinations? Don't just sit there in your room, interpreting the world – it is necessary to change it.' So I ask myself what does 'changing the world' mean, and, supposing that we can, what are the necessary means. This analysis establishes that there is a subjective relation between the existence of a response to the question 'how to change the world?' and real happiness. This relation is established by valorizing the profound sense of the words 'world', 'to change', and 'how', an enterprise that demonstrates in passing that there is nothing, in the question considered, that can disconcert, or that can render the philosopher useless – quite the contrary.

The fourth and final movement is more subjective. It is a question of giving a local example of the strategies and affects of philosophy, the current stage of the course of my philosophical writing-thought. I recapitulate – without losing sight of the bond between truth and happiness – the anterior stages of my work, between *Theory of the Subject* (1982) and *Logics of Worlds* (2006) in passing by *Being and Event* (1988), and therefore the putting in place of the fundamental categories that are being-multiple, the event, truths, and the subject. I then indicate the remaining problems, singularly tied to the question of the 'subject of truth' grasped in the immanence of its act, and therefore what constitutes in some way 'from the interior' its singular happiness. Without disguising the extreme difficulty of what will be the heart of the new book, titled *The Immanence of Truths*, I announce the line to be followed: essentially that of a new dialectic between the finite and the infinite. Happiness can be defined as *the affirmative experience of an interruption of finitude*.

This short little book clears the way, so that the philosophical strategist can say to everyone: 'Here's what you need to convince you that thinking against opinions and in the service of some truths, far from being the unrewarding and pointless exercise you imagine it to be, is the shortest route to true life, which, when it exists, is signalled by an incomparable happiness'.

1

Philosophy and the Desire of Philosophy

As many readers know – Rancière and his friends once gave this title to the wonderful journal they founded – Rimbaud uses a strange expression: 'logical revolts'. Philosophy is something like this: a logical revolt. It is the combination of a desire for revolution – real happiness demanding that one rise up against the world as it is and against the dictatorship of established opinions – *and* of a rational exigency, the revolutionary drive being incapable of achieving alone the goals it sets itself.

Philosophical desire is indeed, very generally speaking, the desire for a revolution in thought and in existence – as much collective existence as personal existence – and with the aim of a real happiness, distinguished from that semblance of happiness which is satisfaction. True philosophy is not an abstract exercise. Since Plato, it has taken a stand against the injustice of the world. It rises up against the miserable state of the world and human life. But it does all this in a movement that always protects the rights of argumentation and which, in the end, proposes a new logic in the same movement by which it disengages the real of happiness from its semblance.

Mallarmé offers us this aphorism: 'All thought emits a throw of the dice.' It seems to me that this enigmatic formula applies equally to philosophy. The fundamental desire of philosophy is to think and realize the universal, among other things because a happiness that is not universal, which excludes the possibility of being shared by every other human animal capable of becoming its subject, is not a real happiness. But this desire is not the result of necessity. It exists in a movement that is always a wager, a risky engagement. In this engagement of thought, the part of chance remains indelible.

We thus draw from poetry the idea that there are four fundamental dimensions of desire that characterize philosophy, especially insofar as it is oriented towards the universality of happiness: the dimensions of revolt, logic, universality and risk.

And is this not the general formula of a desire for revolution? The revolutionary desires that the people rise up; that they do so in an effective and rational fashion, and not in barbarism and rage; that this uprising has an international, universal value, and is not limited by a national, racial or religious identity; finally, the revolutionary assumes the risk, the chance, the favourable circumstance, that often happens only once. Revolt, logic, universality, risk: these are the components of the desire for revolution; these are the components of the desire of philosophy.

But I think that the contemporary world, our world, sometimes called the 'Western' world, exerts a strong negative pressure on the four dimensions of such a desire.

First, our world is a world in part inappropriate or inappropriable for revolt: not that there isn't any, but because what the world teaches or pretends to teach is that it is, in its realized form, already a free world; or a world for which liberty is the organizing value; or, again, a world such that there is no place for wanting or hoping for better (in a radical sense). Therefore this world declares that it has arrived, with imperfections (that one makes an effort to correct), at the threshold of its internal, intimate liberation. And that, in sum, regarding happiness, it is that from which we can expect the best propositions and the best guarantees. But, as this world simultaneously standardizes and commercializes the stakes of this freedom, the freedom that it proposes is a freedom captive to that which it is destined by the network of the circulation of commodities. Thus it is not ultimately appropriate either to the idea of revolting to be free (an antique, ancient theme, the very signification of all revolt) since, in a certain fashion, freedom is proposed by the world itself; nor is it any more appropriate for what one could call a free use of this freedom, since freedom is coded or precoded in the infinite shimmer of commodity production and in what monetary abstraction institutes on that basis.

This is why this world has, in regard to revolts or the possibility of revolt, a disposition that one could call an insidiously oppressive disposition. Whence its proposition regarding happiness is already suspect of latent corruption.

Secondly, this world is inappropriate for logic, principally because it is submitted to the illogical dimension of communication. Communication and its material organization transmit images, statements, words and commentaries, whose assumed principle is incoherence. Communication, in order to establish the reign of its circulation, undoes, day after day, every bond and every principle in a sort of untenable and unbound juxtaposition of all the elements that it carries. One can also say that communication proposes to us in an instantaneous way a spectacle without memory; and that, from this point of view, what it more essentially undoes is a logic of time.

This is why we will maintain that our world is a world that exerts a strong pressure upon thought in its principle of consistency, and that, in a certain fashion, it instead proposes to thought a sort of imaginary dispersion. But one can show – we will do it, but in truth everyone knows it – that real happiness is of the order of concentration, of intensification, and cannot tolerate what Mallarmé called 'these latitudes of indeterminate waves in which all reality dissolves'.[1]

Thirdly, this world is inappropriate for the universal, for two correlative reasons. First, the true material form of its universality is monetary abstraction or the general equivalent. In money resides the only effective sign of everything that is universally circulated and exchanged universally. Next, because,

---

[1] S. Mallarmé, 'Un coup de dés' in *Collected Poems*, trans. with commentary H. Weinfield (Berkeley, Los Angeles and London: University of California, 1994), trans. p. 142.

as we know, this world is at the same time a specialized and fragmentary world, organized in the general logic of productive specializations and in the encyclopaedia of knowledges such that only a slim fragment is able to be mastered. Simultaneously proposing an abstract and monetary form of the universal, and burying under this form a specialized and fragmentary reality, this world exerts a strong pressure upon the very theme of the universal, in the sense that philosophy understands it. Suffice it to say that its 'happiness' is reserved for defined groups and competitive individuals, who won't hesitate to defend it as an inherited privilege, against the mass of those who don't benefit from it in any way.

And, finally, this world is inappropriate for the wager, for the risky decision, because it is a world where nobody any longer has the means to deliver their existence to chance. The world, such as it is, is a world in which the necessity to calculate security reigns supreme. Nothing is more striking in this regard than the fact that teaching, for example, is organized in such a way that the necessary prioritization of the calculation of professional security and its adjustment to the dispositions of the job market is increasingly important. And thus, in a certain way, it is very early taught that the figure of the risky decision must be revoked and suspended, to the profit of an evermore premature calculation of a security, which, moreover, proves itself uncertain in reality. Our world delivers life over to the meticulous and mandatory calculation of this doubtful security, and orders successive sequences of existence according to this calculation. But who doesn't know that real happiness is incalculable?

I would therefore say that the philosophical desire for a revolution of existence, if we conceive of it as this knot of revolt, logic, universality and risk, encounters in the contemporary world four principal obstacles, four mandatory pressures, that are the reign of the commodity, the reign of communication, monetary universality and technical and productive specialization, all subjectively tied by the calculation of personal security.

Capitalism and commodities, techniques of anarchic communication, the limitless authority of monetary circulation, the obsession with security – such are the major obstacles that the contemporary world sets up in opposition to the deployment of the desire for revolution in all its forms. These obstacles aim to reduce the ineluctable idea of the true life, of happiness, to the semblance of a consumer satisfaction.

How can philosophy rise to this challenge? Can it do so? Is it capable of it?

In sketching a response, let us radically simplify the global philosophical situation. We distinguish three principal currents.

First, there is the phenomenological and hermeneutical current, a current which goes back to German Romanticism and whose principal contemporary figures, in the broad sense, are Heidegger and Gadamer. Second, there is the analytic current, which began with the Vienna Circle, with Wittgenstein and Carnap, and which today dominates all English and American university philosophy. And, third, there is the postmodern current which borrows from the two others, and which has undoubtedly been most active in France, inasmuch as we can link it to Jacques Derrida or Jean-François Lyotard. Of course, there are, at the heart of these three fundamental orientations, innumerable mixtures, intersections, knots and common parts, but I believe that these have the merit of sketching a sort of tolerable cartography of the state of things. What interests us here is how each current designates or identifies the desire of philosophy and its possible creative effects in the real world; therefore, what is for each current the definition, explicit or latent, of the true life, whose affect is real happiness.

The hermeneutic current assigns to philosophy the aim of deciphering the sense of existence and thought, and one can say that its central concept is that of interpretation. There are words, acts, configurations, historical destinies whose sense is obscure, latent, hidden, veiled, unrevealed. A method of interpretation will seek a clearing of this obscurity and attempt to bring out a primordial sense that is a figure of our destiny in its relation to the destiny of being itself. If the essential operator is that of interpretation, it is evident that it is a question of unveiling or of opening to an inaugurally inapparent sense. The fundamental opposition for hermeneutic philosophy is that between the closed and the open. The destiny of philosophy is to hold itself in the opening to latent sense and, consequently, to disencumber or disoccupy thought of its recession in the closure, latency and obscurity of its sense. *Revolutionary desire, in thought, is that of a clearing. And real happiness is a subjective figure of the Open.*

The analytic current assigns to philosophy the aim of a strict delimitation between statements that have sense, or which are provided with sense, and statements that don't have it; between what one has the right to say and what is impossible to say; between what can make a consensus around a shared sense and what is incapable of it. Here the major instrument is not interpretation, but the grammatical and logical analysis of statements themselves: this is, moreover, why this current has largely had recourse to the heritage of logic, including its mathematical form. It is a question of a study of the laws and resources of language, the central concept this time being the rule. Drawing out the rule that authorizes the agreement about sense is in the end the essential concern of philosophical activity. We could say that the most important opposition here is not that between the closed and the open, but the opposition between the ruled and the unregulated, between what conforms to a recognized law and what, subtracted from every law as unidentifiable according to a rule, is necessarily illusion and discordance. The aim of philosophy, from this perspective, is therapeutic and critical. It is a question of exposing the illusions that divide us, the non-sense that fosters division and opposition. *Revolutionary desire, in thought, is that of a democratic division of sense. And real happiness is the affect of democracy.*

Finally, the postmodern current assigns to philosophy the aim of deconstructing the received truths of the modern world. It is not a question, this time, of bringing out a latent sense, nor of delimiting sense from non-sense. It is a question of showing that the very question of sense must be otherwise disposed, and, consequently, of deconstructing its anterior figure, of dissolving the great constructions that were – particularly in the nineteenth century and previously – the idea of the historical subject, the idea of progress, the idea of revolution, the idea of humanity; of showing that there is an irreducible plurality of registers and languages in thought as in action, a plurality that does not allow itself to be reabsorbed or unified in a totalizing problematic of sense. Centrally, the objective of postmodern thought is to deconstruct the idea of totality, through which philosophy itself is put in question, destabilized – in such a way that the postmodern current instead stimulates what we can call mixed or impure practices. It situates thought on the edges or on the margins, in the incisions. And, above all, the postmodern current will place the legacy of philosophical thought within a play that ties it to the destiny of art. *Revolutionary desire is finally that of inventing new forms of life, and real happiness is nothing other than the* jouissance *of these forms.*

What now interests us is to ask if there are traits common to these three dominant orientations. We ask if, in the way that they take up the challenge that the world opposes to the desire of philosophy, they follow, on such or such a point, parallel or comparable routes.

There is straightaway a very important negative trait. These three currents announce the end of metaphysics, and, therefore, in some way, the end of philosophy itself, at least in its classical sense or, as Heidegger would say, in its destinal sense. For Heidegger, there is a closure of the history of metaphysics. Philosophy is incapable of moving itself forward in the element of metaphysics. And this closure is also the closure of an entire epoch of the history of being and thought. One can also say that for the ideal of truth, which organizes classical philosophy under

a traditional definition of a 'search for the truth', there is substi-
tuted the idea of a plurality of sense. I am profoundly convinced
that the current pass of philosophy organizes itself around
the decisive opposition between truth, the central category of
classical philosophy (or, if you like, of metaphysics), and the
question of sense, supposed to be the question that occurs in
modernity just where the classical question of truth is closed.

For the hermeneutic current, truth is a category of
metaphysics, which must be taken up in the direction of a
destinal sense of being. The world is composed of an interlacing
of interpretations that no transcendent being is able to oversee.
The coming reign of the open delivers us from the abstract
univocity that represents the true idea.

For the analytic current, it is clearly necessary to abandon the
grand design of a 'search for truth'. The sole point of departure
is the configuration of statements. Sense itself is relative to the
grammar of reference. When you want to delimit sense from
non-sense, it is always necessary to refer to the universe of rules
in which you are operating. There are consequently several
senses or several regimes of sense, which are incomparable, and
this is precisely what Wittgenstein named 'language games'. The
plurality of language games is expressly opposed to the idea of a
transparent recollection under the sign of truth.

Lastly, the postmodern current deconstructs the traditional
support of truths, or that for which there is truth, to which
philosophy had traditionally given the name of subject. One can
say that an essential axis of the postmodern current takes it upon
itself to deconstruct, insofar as it is a product of metaphysics, the

category of subject. There is therefore no subject for whom or for what, or on the basis of whom or of what, there would be truth. There are only occurrences, cases, disparate happenings, and there are genres of discourse, themselves heterogeneous, to gather these disparate cases.

Finally, hermeneutics, analytic, and postmodern philosophy organize a triple opposition between sense – open and plural, symbol of modernity – and the idea of univocal truth – held to be metaphysical and archaic, even 'totalitarian'. This is the common negative trait.

Positively, now, there is a very striking common trait: the central importance of language. It is really through and within the tendencies of these three currents that what one could call the great linguistic turn of Western philosophy was produced. This central place of language, which, again, will be organized or disposed in a differentiated way in the three currents, is perhaps their most obvious common trait. For the hermeneutic current, of course, interpretation, interpretative activity, operates principally on the basis of speech acts, acts of signification, and language is, as the last resort, the very site where the question of the open is decided. It is here, and nowhere else, that is, 'on the way to language' – 'language' preceding understanding in the system of interpretation – that our disposition for thought is accomplished. For the analytic current, statements are the primary material, and, at the end of the day, philosophy is a sort of generalized grammar under the sign of the force of the rule; what exist are sentences, fragments, or types of discourse. Finally, postmodern deconstruction is a linguistic and scriptural action directed against the stability of metaphysical abstractions. The three currents thus place the question of language at the absolute centre of philosophy as such; regardless of whether it is a question of interpretation, of the rule or of deconstruction in the guise of the opposition between speech and writing, one has finally an assumption of language as what one could call the great historical transcendental of our time. We can say, consequently, in order to simplify things, that contemporary philosophy in its main tendencies sustains two axioms, such is its constitutive logic:

- first axiom: the metaphysics of truth has become impossible;
- second axiom: language is the crucial place of thought because it is there that the question of sense is decided.

These two axioms organize in their manner the opposition that is the essential pass of the philosophical question today: namely the relationship between sense and truth.

To come to my own position, I will say that in these two axioms – the impossibility of the metaphysics of truth and the constituting character of the question of language – there is a great danger, that of the incapacity of philosophy to sustain its own desire, on the basis of these axioms, against the pressure that the contemporary world exerts over this desire. The danger is, in sum, of losing all revolutionary virtue, and in this way abandoning the motif of the true life and therefore happiness, to the profit alone of the doctrine of satisfaction, at once individualistic and identitarian.

If philosophy is centrally a meditation on language, if it sets itself up in the plurality of language games and their grammarian codifications, it will never manage to shift the obstacle that the world pits against universality, through its specialization, its fragmentation, and its abstraction. Because there are as many languages as there are communities and activities. Language games are in effect the rule of the world, and we know how difficult it is to circulate between these games. That language games are the law of our world precisely interdicts – inasmuch as philosophy proposes, against the law of the world, a revolution in thought – that these games be the place where the philosophical imperative is formed. Or, and this can be worse, if it is happy to install itself in this primacy of language, philosophy will have to designate one language as that alone which saves it. We know that Heidegger was, in part, engaged upon this route from the moment that he announced the privileged position of the German language as such, in its capacity to give shelter to the open, and from the fact that it was the language that came in this regard to take up the baton of the Greek language. But, by installing ourselves in the plurality of language games and their rules, or in stating the radical privilege of a singular language as that in which lies the authenticity of sense, we do not take up the challenge that the contemporary world opposes to the vocation of philosophy for the universal.

Since Plato, in the *Cratylus*, philosophy has had the task of beginning not from words, but, insofar as it could, from things themselves. I think that this imperative is in effect a trans-temporal imperative of philosophy, and that the whole question is precisely to know how we can start not from language, but from things themselves. Analytic philosophy has privileged, in a unilateral fashion, languages of a scientific type, that is, those that were the most immediately appropriable to logical rules. And it made these languages paradigms of the delimitation of sense, because, as we know, in scientific languages the rule is explicit, whereas in most other languages it remains implicit. But, there again, the unilateral and paradigmatic privilege of languages where the rule is explicit does not permit us to sustain the challenge opposed to universality, for the reason that nothing indicates to us *a priori* that universality necessarily goes hand in hand with the explicit character of rules. This should be proven on its own accord, but it is not when the rule alone gives the law regarding the question of the delimitation of sense.

If, moreover, the category of truth is abandoned or inoperative, philosophy cannot face up to the challenge of an existence in servitude to commodity circulation or to the illogicality of communication. Because – this is a difficult point, but one of which I am profoundly convinced – to the infinite shimmering of commodity circulation, to this sort of flexible plurality in which desire finds itself enchained, we can only oppose the halting point of an exigency that would be unconditional. All that in this world is under condition falls under the law of the circulation of objects, money and images. And interrupting this principle of circulation – to my mind a radical exigency of contemporary philosophy and the primary condition of a route towards real happiness – is only possible insofar as one is in a position to state, or assume, that there is an unconditional halting point; that is, a strategic Idea absolutely antagonistic to this circulation and to its subjectivity, which is both egotistical and ignorant. This strategic Idea has been called for two centuries the communist Idea, and we have hardly begun to glimpse its impact, despite the epico-tragic experiences that incarnated it for a time – several decades of the twentieth century – far too short a time to draw any conclusion at all. At least for those not in a huge hurry to become, or to rebecome, apologists for the market order.

But, on a more abstract or less immediately political level, I think that, with regard to the mediatic inconsistency of images and commentaries, we can only put forward the thesis according to which there exist at least some truths here, and that the persistent research of these truths, beneath the shimmering surface of what is being dealt and circulated, is the imperative to which philosophy must submit if it does not want itself to be engaged and dismembered by the inconsistency of communication.

I will ask, finally, the following question: what sense would there be in wagering on existence, in subtracting it from the imperative of the calculation of personal security, in throwing the dice against routines, in exposing oneself to an arbitrary chance, if it is not in the minimal name of a fixed point, of a truth, of an Idea, or of a value, that prescribes us this risk? And without this point of support, how to imagine the generic form of the happiness of a Subject, whatever it be? Confronted with the wager and by the occurrence of chance by which existence engages in its own novelty, it is therefore ineluctable and necessary to have a fixed point for shelter and support. To maintain the four dimensions of the desire of philosophy (revolt, logic, universality and risk) against the four obstacles that the contemporary world opposes to them (commodities, communication, monetary abstraction and obsession with security), it is thus necessary that we go beyond the three dominant philosophical orientations: the analytic, the hermeneutic, the postmodern. In these three options there is in effect something too suited to the world as it is, something that exaggeratedly reflects the physiognomy of the world itself. And, thus enlisted by these options, organized by them, philosophy tolerates, accepts, the law of this world, without realizing that this law ultimately demands the disappearance of its desire.

My proposition is thus to break with these frames of thought, to rediscover or constitute in renewed configurations a style or a philosophical path that is not that of interpretation, nor that of grammarian analysis, nor that of edges, equivocations and deconstructions. It is a question of rediscovering a foundational, decisive philosophical style, in the school of what was the philosophical style and classical foundation of a Descartes, for example. Of course, neither is it a question of giving in this introduction anything more than a preliminary overview of what the deployment could be of a philosophy that would sustain the challenge of the world in preserving the radicality of its own desire. For this, read my great philosophical treatises: *Being and Event* and *Logics of Worlds*, or in any case their outlines, *Manifesto for Philosophy* and *Second Manifesto for*

Philosophy. But I would like, all the same, to indicate two orientations, or two themes.

First, I will propose that language is not the absolute horizon of thought. Certainly language, or a language, is always the historical body of a philosophy. There is a singular figure of incarnation, a tonality, a colour that reflects the horizon of the language. But I propose that the organization in thought of philosophy is not the immediate tributary of the linguistic rule in which it operates. And, in this regard, one restores the idea that philosophy is universally transmissible. The idea of universal transmissibility was named by Jacques Lacan the idea of the matheme. Let us appropriate it for what we say here. Holding on to the ideal of universal transmission, we say that the ideal of philosophy must be, in effect, the matheme. The matheme is addressed to all, it is universally transmissible, it traverses linguistic communities and the heterogeneity of language games, without privileging any of them; accepting the plurality of their exertions, but without itself traversing or establishing itself in this multiplicity. It will no longer align itself with the formal ideal of scientific language: it will construct in its own element its own figure of universality.

Second, I will propose that the proper, irreducible, singular role of philosophy is to establish a fixed point in discourse: more precisely, to find or propose a name or a category for such a fixed point. In my own philosophical disposition, I have taken up the old word 'truth', but the word hardly matters; what counts is the capacity for some philosophical proposition to establish an unconditioned of this order. Our world is marked by speed and incoherence. Philosophy must be what allows us to say – the moment always comes where we have to be able to say – through a sort of interruption or caesura of this speed or this incoherence that *this* is good and *that* is not. Establishing this point, by means of which we can speak like this, is a task more necessary than ever in philosophy. It is therefore necessary, to my mind, to reconstruct philosophically, without restoration and without archaisms, by the trial of a modern eventality, the category of truth, and, by way of consequence, that of the subject. It will be necessary to do it in such a way that it is not a question of a restoration of metaphysics, but of a redefinition or redeployment of philosophy itself, in a categorical element that authorizes the thought of the fixed point.

One very important task is that, under these conditions, philosophy must have the deceleration of thought as its vocation, to establish its own time. In its own contemporary tendencies, philosophy exhausts itself by following the speed of the world. It is the prisoner of modern times, a time simultaneously hacked-up, segmented and rapid. The vocation of philosophy, inasmuch as it is capable of it, is to establish a time that gives itself time; that is to say, a thought that is a time that gives itself the time of the slowness of investigation and architectonics. This construction of a proper time is, to my mind, the guiding principle of the form that one can demand of philosophy today. There again, the most ordinary experience comes to our aid: to be master of one's time, has this not always been a condition of happiness? Is it not what the masters have always refused to the mass of the dominated? Have not wages – which communism proposed to get rid of *for* humanity – always been represented as an unhappy condition precisely because they are the violent imposition of a heterogeneous time? Have not the workers' revolts regularly challenged the punch card and the timekeeper, the controller, the rhythms? All real happiness supposes a liberation of time.

In numerous contemporary currents, especially in the hermeneutic current and, even more still, in the postmodern current, there is a promotion or a praise of the fragmentary disposition of philosophical discourse. This promotion is rooted in particular in a Nietzschean model. I think that, for reasons of circumstance or opportunity, quite simply because the world imposes it on us, we have to return a principle of continuity to philosophy. Because, at bottom, the fragment is a modality by which philosophical discourse blindly submits itself to the fragmentation of the world itself, and by which, after a certain fashion, through its fragmentary segmentation, it allows monetary and market abstraction to represent the only principle of continuity. It is therefore indispensable that philosophy develop its own intrinsic slowness and restore the continuity of thought: namely, both the principle of decision that founds it, and the rational time that binds it.

Let us now ask if under these same conditions there is a chance to see philosophy, evidently in peril, succeed in sustaining the challenge of which we spoke at the beginning, that is, sustaining its desire. Philosophy is sick, this is not in doubt, and the blows it suffers are always correlative with internal difficulties. It seems to me – and these will be the reasons for optimism that I advance – that to this sick person who, in a certain sense, never stops claiming himself sicker than he can say, to this sick person who announces his imminent death and even that it's already come, to this sick person, the contemporary world – the world, at least a part of this world – at the same time that it exerts an indistinct pressure to break his desire, paradoxically demands that he live. As always, the sense of the world is equivocal. For one part, the general system of circulation, communication, security, is oriented towards weakening the desire of philosophy. However, paradoxically, it creates, it organizes in a contradictory fashion, in its own interior, a question that is addressed vaguely and like a void to the possibility of philosophy. Why is this?

First of all, there is the growing conviction – growing in any case with those who attempt to exist in the autonomy of their own thought – that the human sciences are not, or will not be, in any state to replace philosophy, both in its disciplinary disposition and in the singular nature of its desire. There was a time when a widespread idea, one of the figures of the theme of the end of philosophy, was that a sort of general anthropology, normed by the ideal of science – subsuming sociology, economy, political theory, linguistics, 'scientific' psychology, even psychoanalysis – could be assumed to substitute for philosophy: another way of saying that we had arrived at the end of philosophy. I believe for my part that it now appears that the human sciences deploy themselves as a place of statistical means, general configurations, and that they do not truly permit the treating or broaching of the singular, the singularity, in thought. But singularity, if one thinks about it carefully, is always the proper site of decision; and every decision, ultimately, as a veritable decision, is a singular decision. There is not, properly speaking, any general decision, and, inasmuch as what engages a truth, or engages with a truth, or sustains a fixed point, is of the order of decision, it is always also of the order of singularity. We will therefore ask if it is possible today to formulate a philosophy of singularity that is thus also capable of being a philosophy of decision and of risk.

Secondly, everyone has, in effect, noted the ruin of the great collective subjects, a ruin, there again, in thought. It is not so much a question of knowing if these subjects existed, exist, or will exist, but a question of the fact that the great categories that permitted the apprehension of the collective subject seem today to be saturated and incapable of truly animating thought, whether it concerns figures of the historical progress of humanity, or of large class subjects – such as the proletariat – conceived as objective realities. This alerts everyone to what I would call the necessity of deciding and speaking in one's own name, even and above all when it is a question of responding to what the upsurge of a new truth demands of everyone. But evidently the necessity of deciding and speaking in one's own name, even and above all when the question is political, demands this decision, a fixed point, an unconditional principle, a shared Idea that supports and universalizes the primitive decision. It is necessary that each person, in her own name, but open to the organized sharing of her speech with others, can pronounce that *this* is true, *that* is false, or that this is good, that is bad. If, therefore, a philosophy of singularity is required of us, what is also required of us, in this sense, is a philosophy of truth.

Thirdly, we are contemporary with an expansion of communitarian, religious, racist and nationalist passions. This expansion is evidently the other side of the destruction of the great rational configurations of the collective subject. From the weakening and collapse of these great configurations, from the absence, temporary but unfortunate, of the communist Idea, the result has been that a sort of obscure sludge has emerged, that imaginarizes [imaginaries] the totalities of change, to precisely avoid having to pronounce or decide in one's own name, and which essays to hand itself over, according to protocols of delimitation, exclusion and antagonism, to archaic subjects, whose return becomes more and more threatening. In this regard, it is absolutely clear that philosophy is enjoined to give a rational figure to a fixed point or to the unconditioned which it has to support, and by showing that it is not because there is a defection of anterior rational configurations of collective historical destiny that one should abandon the virtue of the rational consistency of thought. Philosophy is therefore also asked what capacity it has to propose a renewed figure, a foundational figure of rationality that would be homogenous to the contemporary world.

Finally – this is the last thing – everyone has a heavy consciousness that the world as we know it is an extraordinarily precarious world. There is moreover a paradox, because it presents itself in a certain sense as the best of possible worlds, it being understood that every other world, those attempted under the paradigm of revolution or emancipation, proved to be at once criminal and ruinous. But, at the same time, this world, presented as the best of possible worlds, is a world that knows itself to be extraordinarily vulnerable. It is an exposed world. It is not at all a world established in the durable stability of its being. It is a world that hardly knows itself and that entrusts itself to too-abstract laws in order not to be exposed to the catastrophe of events it would not know how to receive or welcome. As it happens, war has ravaged entire countries for fifty years without interruption, and it prowls more and more about the immediate neighbourhoods of 'Western' egotism.

In regard to this dangerous vulnerability of the world that proposes at every moment, beyond its general law of circulation and communication, all kinds of unnameable strangeness and dispersed monstrosities, in regard to this world that could finally very well be overturned from one moment to another – here or there, or finally everywhere, in violence, war or oppression, in a species of blindness to itself that is very striking – I think philosophy is asked to be capable of welcoming or thinking the event itself, not so much the structure of the world, the principle of its laws or the principle of its closure, but how the event, surprise, requisition, and precariousness can be thinkable in a still-rational configuration.

This is why, at the price of a certain rupture with the hermeneutic, the analytic and the postmodern, I think that what is asked of philosophy, from the interior of the infinite precariousness of this world, is to take the risk of a determined, foundational philosophy, that is at the same time a philosophy of singularity, a philosophy of truth, a rational philosophy, and a philosophy of the event. What is demanded is therefore to propose, as a shelter or envelope of the desire of philosophy, what one could call a rational knot of singularity, of the event, and of truth. This knot must invent a new figure of rationality, because everyone knows that the knotting of singularity and event to truth is, as such, in the classical tradition, a paradox. It is precisely this paradox that contemporary philosophy must treat centrally if it wishes to work in defence of its own desire and repeat in a constructive and generalized fashion for the whole of humanity the notorious aphorism of Saint-Just: 'happiness is a new idea in Europe'.

For my part, what I have tried to show elsewhere is that the rational knot of singularity, event and truth constitutes by itself a new possible doctrine of the subject. Against the idea that the subject co-belongs to metaphysics and must be deconstructed as so belonging, I say that, insofar as the subject is conceived precisely as the ultimate differential where singularity, event, and truth are rationally knotted, one can and must propose to thought and to the world a new figure of the subject, whose maxim would be the following: a subject is singular because it is always an event that constitutes it in a truth. Or again: a subject is at once a place of possible rationality and what one could call the point of truth of the event. Finally, there is no happiness except for a subject, insofar as an individual accepts becoming subject.

These theses are in some way only the formal diagonal of the philosophical enterprise of which I have tried here to give the grounds or the programme.

If one considers the things of thought and the world on the basis of a philosophy of this kind, a philosophy for which the singularity of the subject comes from an event that constitutes it in a truth, we can say that, in a certain sense, metaphysics is ruined or finite, but in no way that the categories of metaphysics are wholly obsolete. We will thus also say, always relying on such a philosophy, that certainly metaphysics is ruined, but that the deconstruction of metaphysics is itself also ruined and that the world needs a founding philosophical proposition, one which is established on the mixed or conjoined ruins of metaphysics and the dominant figure of the critique of metaphysics.

For all these reasons, I believe that the contemporary world has more need of philosophy than philosophy itself believes. All this is not surprising, if one makes the diagnosis that the dominant currents of contemporary philosophy are too suited to the law of the world. And, that, too well suited to the law of the world, they failed to tell us what true life can be. At the end of the day, what this same world asks from philosophy is, for these currents, an in-apparent part. To render it apparent, there must be an interruption in philosophy itself, that is to say an interruption by the proposal that it keeps to its real task.

The maxim could be: to end with the end. And to end with the end supposes that a decision be taken. No end ends by itself, the end does not end, the end is interminable. To put an end to the end, to finish with the end, it is necessary that a decision be made. Regarding this decision, I have tried to give precisely, at once, the points of support and the elements of validation for what is asked of philosophy by the world itself.

I do not at all deny that philosophy is sick; perhaps even after all, in regard to the fullness of the programme and the difficulty of sustaining it, it is perhaps even dying. But the world is saying, the world is saying to this dying being, without there being need of sending for a saviour or a miracle – this at least is my hypothesis – the world is saying to this dying being: 'Get up and walk!' To walk, then, under the imperative of a true Idea, destines us to happiness.

2

Philosophy and Antiphilosophy Put to the Test of Happiness

I call 'antiphilosopher' that particular kind of philosopher who opposes the drama of his existence to conceptual constructions, for whom the truth exists, absolutely, but must be encountered, experienced, rather than thought or constructed. This is how we must understand Kierkegaard, when he says that all truth is 'in interiority', or, again, that 'subjectivity itself is the distinctive sign of the truth'. But be careful! The antiphilosopher is in no way a sceptic or a relativist, a contemporary democrat, partisan of the diversity of cultures, of that variegation of opinions which, as Deleuze wrote to me shortly before dying, has 'no need' of the idea of truth. On the contrary, the antiphilosopher is the hardest, most intolerant of believers. See Pascal, Rousseau, Nietzsche, Wittgenstein: imperious, implacable personalities, engaged against the 'philosophers' in a merciless struggle. Descartes, for Pascal? 'Useless and uncertain'. Voltaire, Diderot, Hume, for Rousseau? Corrupt, conspirers. The philosopher, for Nietzsche? The 'criminal of criminals', to be shot without delay. The conceptions of rational metaphysics for Wittgenstein? Pure and simple non-sense. And, for Kierkegaard, the majestic Hegelian construction? A geriatric's absence from the world: 'The philosopher is outside; he is not a participant. He sits and grows old listening to the songs of the past; he has an ear for the harmonies of mediation.'[1]

This fury of thought, indexed to an inflexible vision of personal life, is served with all the great antiphilosophers with a style that cannot be separated from their vision. It isn't much to say that they are great writers! Pascal and Rousseau revolutionized French prose, Nietzsche drew unknown accents from the German language. Wittgenstein's *Tractatus* compares only to Mallarmé *Coup de dés*, and Lacan, whom I have demonstrated to be, for the moment, the last truly considerable antiphilosopher, assigns psychoanalysis to an invented language.

The philosopher that I am – conceptual, systematic, infatuated by the matheme – can evidently not cede to the song of these marvellous and carnivorous sirens that are the antiphilosophers. But there is a duty to think to the height of the challenge they represent. As Ulysses, attached to the solid mast of what is

---

[1] S. Kierkegaard, *Either/Or, Part II*, ed. and trans. H. V. Hong and E. H. Hong with intro. and notes (Princeton: Princeton University Press, 1987), pp. 171–2. Trans. mod.

in play in the thought of the Absolute after Plato, he must hear them, understand them, and impose upon himself the duties to which their acrimony recalls him, for, without them, he would become a consensual democrat, a propagandist of a seemly little happiness, and an adept of the imperative 'Live without Idea'.

What impassions me, in these violent and superb adversaries, is the following: against the contractual and deliberative moderation inflicted upon us today as a norm, they recall that the subject has no chance to hold itself at the height of the Absolute except in the tense and paradoxical element of choice. One must wager, says Pascal; one must encounter in oneself, says Rousseau, the voice of conscience; and Kierkegaard, 'through the choice, [the subject] submerges itself in that which is being chosen, and when it does not choose, it withers away'.[2] And, in regard to real happiness, it is subordinated to the chancy encounters which summon us to choose. It is here that the true life appears, or, if we weaken, disappears, hardly glimpsed.

It is a question of life or death, the wager, the choice, the imperious decision. The subject exists only in this test, and no happiness is conceivable if the individual does not surmount the web of mediocre satisfactions in which it is held by its animal objectivity, to become the Subject of which it is capable – and every individual disposes, more or less secretly, the capacity of becoming Subject.

Whence a fascinating trait: that any episode of life, however trivial or minimal it might be, can be the occasion

---

[2] Kierkegaard, *Either/Or*, p. 163.

for experiencing the Absolute, and therefore real happiness, from the moment that it convokes a pure choice, without prior concept, without rational law, a choice that is, according to Kierkegaard, 'the baptism of the will, which assimilates this into the ethical'.[3] We know the support that Pascal knew how to draw, to the benefit of faith, from sickness. Rousseau can meditate upon a fainting fit, even, about masturbation. When Kierkegaard makes his nuptials with Regine the supreme test in which the passage is played out from the aesthetic stage (the seduction of Don Juan) to the ethical stage (the existential seriousness of marriage), then to the religious stage (the purified and absolutized my-self that I become in choice, beyond despair), he manifests a typical trait of antiphilosophy, which is that ordinary existence, the anonymous individual, can come to, better than the pompous philosopher, the chance of the Absolute. It is in this that the antiphilosopher is a *profound* democrat. He has no concern for titles, qualifications, contracts. Debate, freedom of opinions, respect for the other, voting: he affirms that all this is merely twaddle. On the other hand, anyone is worth anyone regarding the possibility of becoming a subject required by the Absolute. Equality is in this sense radical, without condition. Kierkegaard glorifies the ordinary individual who knows to practise this resignation, this superior passivity, thanks to which the subject cannot have his true life in immediate life, but sees himself signify what he might truly *encounter* in life.

---

[3] Kierkegaard, *Either/Or*, p. 169.

The word 'encounter' is essential. A love, a riot, a poem: these are not deduced, these are not distributed in the consensual serenity of participation, these are encountered, and this violent overturning of immediate life results in a singular access as much to the universal as to the Absolute. All real happiness plays out in a contingent encounter: there is not any necessity to be happy. Only 'democratic' individuals of the contemporary world, those distressed atoms, imagine that one can live in the peace of laws, contracts, multiculturalism, and discussions among friends. They do not see that living is living *absolutely*, and that from then on no comfortable objectivity can guarantee this life. The risk of becoming-subject is necessary, as Kierkegaard teaches us, it is necessary that 'objective uncertainty … [be] held fast in the passion of inwardness, which precisely is the relation of inwardness raised to the highest power'.[4]

Maintaining 'objective uncertainty': this antiphilosophical contestation of the powers of objectivity is a salutary maxim. Why submit yourself to what is, just because it is? Preparing himself to discern the laws of the social contract and the chances of freedom, Rousseau declares (and this is his discourse on method): 'Leave aside all the facts'. He is right. Economic and political 'realism' is a great school of submission. The individual can wallow there; the subject cannot come to be there. Because a subject is born from the incalculable encounter of an unknown

---

[4] Kierkegaard, *Concluding Unscientific Postscript to Philosophical Crumbs*, ed. and trans. A. Hannay (Cambridge: Cambridge University Press 2009), p. 514.

possible, to which is knotted a becoming-Subject, it is the only point of which one can say, as does Pascal: 'joy, tears of joy'.

Every day it is explained to us that the constraints of globalization and modernization, not counting the immutable rules of user-friendly democracy, reasonably oblige us to consent to this or that. The great antiphilosophers can at least help us to elude the traps of consent. Even supposing that turning one's back on them is desperate or absurd, it is highly likely that such is the way of the subject, of the unique irreducible capacity that is its own: moving in the element of truth. Even if, as Kierkegaard states, 'in choosing in the absolute sense', that is, against the injunction of the reasonable and the legal, 'I choose despair', it nevertheless remains the case that 'in despair I choose the Absolute, because I myself am the absolute'.[5] In this sense – and this is why, for the great tormented beings who are the antiphilosophers, happiness is not made for jovial guys – a certain dose of despair is the condition of real happiness.

These gripping formulas remind us that becoming subject of a truth, and thus participating a little in the Absolute, is a chance that existence proposes to us in the modality of an encounter. If, generally, holding oneself in an inflexible fashion to the consequences of this encounter is absurd and contemptible in the eyes of the world as it is, if this soft consensual condemnation makes us despair, nevertheless our own access to what we can be is here put into play, and the subjective way is undoubtedly that of obstinacy, that of pure choice in assuming the consequences

---

[5] Kierkegaard, *Either/Or*, p. 213.

of our rout and reroute [*dé-route*]. It is evidently already this insistence of the reroute that Sartre found in Kierkegaard, to dialecticize a little what nonetheless fascinated him: the grand route of History opened for us by the monumental construction sites of Hegel and Marx.

It is that we would not know to speak of the subject of a truth (amorous, political, artistic, scientific …) without introducing the idea of a creation, even if the *context* of this creation is determined and repetitive (Kierkegaard is at least the greatest thinker of repetition). And creation demands the gap of self to self, the paradoxical existence of a difference in the identical, without the resources of Hegelian mediation. Which Kierkegaard summarizes thus: 'This self [of the subject of the choice] has not existed before, because it came into existence through the choice, and yet it has existed, for it was indeed "himself".'[6]

This is the testimony, exemplary for us, philosophers, of the great antiphilosophers, those bitter sacrificers of the concept: existence is capable of more than its perpetuation. It is capable, in the element of truth, of some subject-effect. And the affect of this effect, whether it be political enthusiasm, scientific beatitude, aesthetic pleasure or amorous joy, is always what merits, beyond every satisfaction of needs, the name of happiness.

Certainly, to shore up their violence or their fantasy, these sacrificers of the concept need religion, God, miserable lives, hatreds, the absurd … But the lesson remains. If you want to become something other than you are ordained to be, have

---

[6] Kierkegaard, *Either/Or*, p. 215.

confidence only in encounters, devote your fidelity to what is officially prohibited, keep yourself on the roads of the impossible. Be re-routed. Then, you might, as the final words of Beckett's sublime text *Ill Seen Ill Said* say, 'know happiness'.[7]

[7] S. Beckett, 'Ill Seen Ill Said' in *Samuel Beckett: Volume IV Poems, Short Fiction, Criticism*, ed. P. Auster, Intro. J. M. Coetzee (New York: Grove Press, 2006), p. 470.

3

To Be Happy, Must
We Change the World?

A great tradition of immemorial Wisdom has it that man must adapt his desires to reality, rather than wish to adapt reality to his desire. In this vision, there is something like a *fatum* of the real, and the highest happiness of which humanity is capable resides in the serene acceptance of the inevitable. Stoic philosophy provides the form for this consistently prevailing 'wisdom', including today, where it claims: the small domestic happiness, the consumer, connectivity and the holiday-maker that capitalism and its 'democracy' offer the privileged citizens of the West, may not be exceptionally intense, but desiring something else, communism for example, inevitably leads to the worst. In this propaganda, the 'realities', essentially economic, impose on us private property and the concentration of Capital as the Destiny to which all our desires must submit.

When Saint-Just, in the midst of the French Revolution, writes that 'happiness is a new idea in Europe', it is to an entirely different vision of things that he calls the human Subject. The Revolution must uproot the old world and establish an essential link between virtue (whose contrary is corruption, invariable resource of the power of the rich) and happiness. That is to say that a complete change of world, an emancipation of all humanity against the oligarchical forms that have invariably dominated, from ancient slavery to imperialist capitalism, is the prerequisite for real happiness being a vital possibility available to all.

During the whole nineteenth century and a good part of the twentieth century, at a global level, the conception that to be happy meant to change the world remained very active. The question at stake in this irresistible current of revolutionary nature is thus: *how* to change the world?

It quickly becomes clear that this is never a simple question, insofar as it contains not less than three very difficult words: the name 'world', the verb 'to change', and the interrogative adverb 'how'. So we are from the outset confronted with a complex grammatical syntagm.

Let us start with the name 'world'. What exactly is a world, or as we usually say, what is 'our world', our contemporary world? If we do not immediately specify what we mean by 'world', the title of this chapter becomes a very obscure question.

Let's take a contemporary example, the famous movement, in 2012, of a fraction of the youth of the United States, a movement given the name 'Occupy Wall Street'. What is the world that this revolt, this uprising, would seek to change? Is it 'Wall Street' as symbol of finance capital? The protestors declared: 'we represent

99 per cent of the population, while Wall Street represents only 1 per cent'. Does this mean that the world against which they protested was, beyond pure economics, the political pretence of democracy in which a small group of rich and powerful people motivated solely by their private interests control the lives of millions and millions of other people? Was their argument that collective happiness is conditional on the end of this 'democracy' in which this small group, this 1 per cent, can decree the absolute misery of millions of people living far from the Western capitals, namely in Asia or Africa? However, we might equally say that the people who occupied Wall Street were principally young men and women of the middle classes. Perhaps they were protesting against that miserable, precarious life, that life without a clear and bright future which is the lot of so many young men and women of our Western world? And, in that case, their question was not so much about 'changing' the world as actively testifying, for a few days or a few weeks, to something false and unhappy in our collective existence. And it is likely, as the result showed, that, behind this hopelessly subjective state of mind, there was no clear picture of the objective world and the principles of its change in the direction of the emancipation of happiness, happiness as a new idea. In truth, what really was and should have become the world remained veiled by the momentary joy of the movement.

This is because 'world' is in no way a simple name. At what level can we begin to talk about the world? It is clear that we must define different levels of generality or existence to understand what a world is. I propose to distinguish five.

Firstly, there is our interior world of representations, of passions, opinions, memories: the world of individuals with their bodies and their minds. Secondly, we can define collective worlds in the form of closed groups: those of my family, my profession, my language, my religion, my culture, or my nation. These worlds are dependent on a fixed identity. We might equally consider the global history of humanity as a world. This is not a closed group or a fixed identity, it is an open process which includes numerous and important differences. Equally, we must take into account our natural context, our inclusion in nature that we share with the stones, the plants, the animals, the oceans, etc. This world is our little planet Earth. And finally, at a fifth level, there are the universe, the stars, the galaxies, the black holes … We have, in short: the world of individuals, which is that of psychology; the world of closed groups, which is that of sociology; the world of the open process, which is the existence of humanity, or History; our natural world, that of biology and ecology; and finally, the universe, the world of physics and cosmology.

Let's turn to the second difficulty, the verb 'to change'. It is clear that our potential or our capacity to change a world is absolutely dependent on the level of definition of this world. If I am married and fall in love with another woman, that can eventually determine a very important change in the first two levels: my individual world – passions, representations, etc. – and my closed family world. And, without doubt, this greatly affects my representation of personal happiness. At the second level, there are numerous types of change: revolution, reforms, civil wars, the creation of new states, the disappearance of a language, colonialism, or even what Nietzsche calls 'the death of God'. Each of these changes corresponds to the identification of new dialectics of happiness and unhappiness.

At the third level, that of History, there are the contrasting notions of progress, internationalism, or communism on one side, and, on the other, capitalism as the end of History, of democracy as a universal objective, and, behind all these prestigious names, objective imperialism and subjective nihilism. These are, as I have said already, the possible frameworks for a philosophy of happiness, whether stoical and resigned, whether revolutionary or militant.

At the fourth level, we have the current and complex debate about environmental problems, climate change and the future of our planet. There is a resource here for the millenarian conception of the happiness of the human species.

At the fifth level, we can't do much. We are only a tiny part, an insignificant fragment of the global universe. But we look for signs of life beyond our miserable planet, and hold out hopes of maybe one day encountering completely new forms of beatitude.

What exactly is the significance of the verb 'to change' in all this? In fact, I think that our distinctions and our definitions are too imprecise to provide a clear sense for the expression 'change the world'. After all, it is not true that a world can change as a totality. You have to see how things work relative to the different semantic levels of the name 'world'. An individual can change his life, but certain parts of his subjective world are invariant, just as certain features of his body or certain fundamental psychic formations are determined by childhood experiences.

We can escape the limitations of our closed groups, but we cannot completely avoid being determined by our origins, our language, and the cultural background of our nationality. The same goes for our actions in an open history or our efforts to modify or preserve our natural environment.

In all these biographical or historical circumstances, the possibility of a local change in a determined world can be observed, after which there can be consequences of this local change – sometimes far-reaching consequences – entailing reorganizations as much in the representation as in the real of happiness. A change never immediately appears in a clear fashion as 'changing the world'. It is counted as big or small relative to this world, and only retroactively, through the consequences it entails.

Take the famous example of the Bolshevik Revolution in Russia in October 1917. The great American journalist, John Reed, wrote an account of this revolution to which he gave the title *Ten Days That Shook the World*. But what world is it? It was certainly not a complete change of the capitalist world, as Marx and Lenin imagined (Lenin was convinced that the Russian Revolution was only the beginning of a global process, whose second stage would be revolution in Germany). Still, this local event had far reaching consequences. It played the role of benchmark for all revolutionary activists and represented a critical part – from the Soviet Union to Communist China, passing by the Vietnam War and Cuba – of 'the world of the twentieth century'. But during the second half of the century we have witnessed the collapse of practically all the 'socialist states' constructed in the wake of the 1917 Bolshevik Revolution. Thus it is only now that we can comprehend the title of John Reed's book. Certainly, a part of the world has been shaken by the Russian Revolution. Certainly, its long-range consequences qualify it as an event of real and considerable change. But, ultimately, our world today is dominated by global capitalism just as it was before this event took place. We could then conclude that the most important political change of the twentieth century did not 'change the world'.

As a consequence, and to understand 'How?', I propose to substitute for the idea 'changing the world' a complex of three terms, three concepts: the event, the real, the consequences. And I will now endeavour to explain as clearly as possible the philosophical terminology as it relates to the generic question of happiness.

The event is the name of something that is locally produced in a world, and which cannot be deduced from the laws of this same world. It is a local rupture in the ordinary becoming of a world. We know that in general the rules of a world produce a sort of repetition of the same process. For example, in the capitalist world, Marx proposed the complete explanation of the repetition of the cycle of the investment of money, of its transformation into goods and its return to money, or the repetitive relation between salaries, price and profit. More generally, he portrays the global process of capital as the relation between production and circulation. He equally proposes a clear explication of the fact that the cyclical crises are not ruptures in the becoming of capitalism but are rational parts of its development.

This is precisely why an event is in no sense a classical crisis. For example, the current economic crisis in Europe is not an event: it is a constitutive part of the globalized capitalist world. An event is something that is produced locally within the globalized capitalist world, but cannot be fully understood if we simply employ the repetitive logic of capital, which comprises the laws of systemic crises.

The force of an event resides in that it exposes something in the world that was hidden, or invisible, because masked by the laws of this world. An event is the revelation of a part of the world which existed previously only in the form of a negative constraint. And the correlation between this revelation and the question of happiness is clear: as it is the lifting of a constraint, there is immediately, for all those who subsist without clearly recognizing this constraint, the apparition of new possibilities for thought and action. Thus a possible definition of happiness might be: to discover in oneself an active capacity of what we unknowingly possess.

I'll give two examples.

Why was May '68 a real event in France? And why, beyond a certain disappointment, beyond what is too conveniently called a revolutionary 'failure', has this event left its actors, at least those that the corruptions of the 1980s have not rendered zombies, the memory of an intense, transfigured, absolutely happy moment – even if anxious – of their existence? The reason is that the simultaneous occurrence of the massive revolt of students and the biggest general strike of factory workers ever seen, in the world 'France of the 1960s,' showed that the strict separation between young intellectuals and young workers as a law of the world was necessarily antiquated. The event revealed precisely that this law could be, and ultimately had to be, replaced by its contrary: a new political current created by the direct unity of young intellectuals and workers. If the French Communist Party was not a positive actor in this affair, but rather a target of the movement, this is because it was also organized according to the law of this separation: any direct relation between the intellectual cells and the cells of communist workers was strictly prohibited. This is why the party was equally a part of the old world. The real of the 'new' world, in the frame of the old world revealed by the event, consisted in the affirmation that a form of political unity, that had been prohibited by all the components of the old world, was possible. And the discovery that it was perfectly possible to construct in society the trajectory of that unity, to break down social barriers, to become equals of a politics that invented itself at the same time it was practised, was the source of a subjective illumination without precedent.

Another illustration of the real force of an event is the famous Tahrir Square during the Arab Spring in Egypt. A relation of indifference at best, of antagonism at worst, between Muslims and Christians was the communal law accepted in the national world of 'Egypt'. But a tight unity between the two communities, as a possible new law of this world, was observed during the occupation of the square by the popular masses. For example, Christians protected Muslims during their prayers, and, more generally, the political slogans were the same for both communities. And, again, even though the historical development was marked by a deadly circularity – the rupture between the educated petty bourgeoisie and the Islamists ended in the military coming back to power – the subjective trace of this time of unity remains as what will inevitably illuminate the future.

In both cases, the new real revealed by the event is in the form of a new unity that goes beyond the differences previously established. But these differences were 'established' in the world as the laws of that world itself. And these laws, as all laws, prescribe what is possible and what is impossible. For example, that the intellectuals and ordinary workers must be separated in everyday life as in collective action or thought. But in fact May '68 affirmed the political possibility of a direct unity of thought, of action and of organization between these two groups. The same thing goes for the relations between Muslims and Christians in Egypt.

All this allows me a crucial observation: thanks to the force of an event, many people discover that the real of the world can be situated in something which is simply impossible from the dominant point of view of this world. We, here, encounter the profound sense of the slogan of May '68 in France: 'Be realistic: demand the impossible!' and we perfectly comprehend the slightly mysterious phrase of Lacan: 'The real is the impossible'.[8]

The new affirmation, the great 'yes' that declares the real of the world under the pressure of an event, is always the promise

---

[8] J. Lacan, *The Other Side of Psychoanalysis: The Seminar of Jacques Lacan, Book XVII*, trans. R. Grigg (New York: W. W. Norton, 2007), *passim*, e.g. p. 123.

of the possibility that something is possible that was previously impossible. And in this sense we can say that *happiness is always the* jouissance *of the impossible.*

What I call the 'consequences of the event' is a concrete process in the world, which develops the different forms of possibility of what was impossible. Thus it is also the executive power of happiness. I call this kind of process a 'fidelity' to the event: in other words, the acts, creations, organizations and thoughts which accept the new and radical possibility of that whose impossibility was a law of the world. We can then say: *all real happiness is a fidelity.*

Being faithful is to become the subject of change, in accepting the consequences of an event. We can also say that novelty always has the appearance of a new subject, whose law is the realization in the world of the new real revealed – *qua* point of impossibility – as a possibility prohibited by the 'old' world. Let us say: *happiness is the coming, in an individual, of the Subject it discovers it can become.*

The new subject exists when people include themselves in the organization, stabilization, and forms capable of tolerating the consequences of an event. On the other hand, the subject is not wholly subject to the laws of the world, because the consequences themselves derive from an event, and the event is a rupture in the ordinary becoming of a world. Thus the new subject is at same time inside and outside the old world. We can say it is immanent to the world, but in the form of an exception. Let's essay, then, that *happiness is the affect of the Subject as immanent exception.*

We can mark three fundamental traits of this new subject, which we can also conceive as the subject of happiness.

Firstly, the freedom of this subject is to create something in the world, but as an exception. A creation of this order accepts the consequences of the fact that the real that has been revealed in the event is opposed to certain negative constraints of this world. Thus the true essence of freedom for this subject is not doing whatever it wants. In fact, 'what you want to do' is itself part of your adaptation to the world as it is. If the world provides for you the means to do what you want, it is surely because you obey the laws of the world as it is. In the case of real creation, you have equally to create some, if not all, the means of your creation. True freedom is always a way of doing what is prescribed by the real as exceptional consequence in the world. Consequently, *the true essence of freedom, essential condition of real happiness, is discipline.* This is why artistic creation can here serve as paradigm. Everyone knows that an artist obeys the strict discipline of innovation: day after day, patient and often gruelling work, in order to achieve or to find the forms for a new representation of the real. This is also of course the case for what concerns scientific innovation. More generally, we must affirm that a subject exists at the point where it is impossible to distinguish between discipline and freedom. The existence of such a point is signalled by an intense happiness, evidenced in particular in poetic expression, which is inseparably language 'in freedom' and strict formal discipline.

Secondly, the subject cannot be closed by an identity. As an immanent exception, the emancipatory process is open and infinite because, being situated to a certain degree outside the constraining limits of the world, the work of a subject is always universal and cannot be reduced to the law of this or that identity. In so being, a work of art, a scientific discovery, a political revolution, a true love interests all humanity. This is why the workers, who have nothing and are reduced to the capacities of their bodies, are in Marx's eyes the generic part of humanity. This absence of identity, this generic negation of identity, equally explains the famous declaration from the *Manifesto of the Communist Party*: 'the workers have no country'. From the objective point of view of the world, a subject, as immanent exception to a world, still has a country. But from the point of view of the process of emancipation, the subject, as immanent exception, is generic and without country. And happiness, we know, by its subjective power, exhausts all identitarian constraint. This is the sense of the formula: 'lovers are alone in the world', which signifies that their own work – love – dis-identifies anything that could distinguish or separate them.

Thirdly, the being-happy of the subject, as I've said, resides in the discovery, from its own interior, of its capacity to do something it did not know it was capable of. The whole point here is the sublation – in the Hegelian sense of *Aufhebung* – namely, passing beyond an apparent limit in discovering within itself the resources for its overcoming. In this sense, all happiness is a victory against finitude.

It is necessary to introduce here a sharp distinction between 'happiness' and 'satisfaction'. I am satisfied when I see that my individual interests are in conformity with what the world has to offer. Satisfaction is thereby determined by the laws of the world and by the harmony between these laws and myself. Ultimately, I am satisfied when I can be assured that I am well integrated with the world. But we can object that satisfaction is in reality a form of subjective death, because the individual, reduced to its conformity with the world as it is, is incapable of becoming the generic subject that it is capable of being.

In a process of emancipation, we experience the fact that happiness is the dialectical negation of satisfaction. Happiness is on the side of affirmation, of creation, of the new, and of genericity. Satisfaction is on the side of what Freud named the death drive, the reduction of subjectivity to objectivity. Satisfaction is the passion of seeking and finding the 'vantage point' [*bonne place*] offered the individual by the world, then remaining there.

That is why this whole text speaks of the close relationship between happiness and subjectivization of a post-evental process of (political) emancipation, (artistic) creation, (scientific) invention or of alteration, in the sense of a becoming-other-in-itself (love).

At this point we can return to the interrogation that constitutes my title: 'How to change the world'?

The response might be: by becoming a subjective part of the consequences of a local event. We could also say: in being faithful to an event, in creating an equivalence between freedom and discipline, in inventing a new form of happiness which is a victory over the dictatorship of satisfaction and the power of the death drive. We know that something is changing in the world when we experience that happiness is not the predetermined objective of the process of change but the creative subjectivization of the process itself. The world is changing when we can declare, as did Saint-Just, that happiness is a new idea.

This vision was fundamental to Marx's conception of revolution. For him, the name of the new possibility of collective justice was, as we know, 'communism'. The negative constraint of capitalism, as revealed by the revolutionary event, is clear: for capitalism, equality is impossible. Consequently, 'communism' is the name of the political possibility of this impossibility: the possibility of equality. But, as we see in the *Manuscripts of 1844* and in the famous *Manifesto*, Marx doesn't think that communism is the programme of a new society or an abstract idea of justice. Communism is the name of the historical process of the destruction of the old society. Thus to change is not to obtain a result. The result lies in the change itself.

Undoubtedly this vision can be interpreted at a more general level: happiness is not the possibility of the satisfaction of everyone. Happiness is not the abstract idea of a good society in which everyone is satisfied. Happiness is the subjectivity of a difficult task: coping with the consequences of an event and discovering, beneath the dull and dreary existence of our world, the luminous possibilities offered by the affirmative real, of which the law of this world was the hidden negation. Happiness is enjoying the powerful and creative existence of something that, from the world's point of view, was impossible.

How to change the world? The response is truly encouraging: by being happy. But we have to pay the price, which is to be really dissatisfied from time to time. It is a choice, the true choice of our lives. It is the true choice concerning the true life.

The French poet, Arthur Rimbaud, wrote: 'The true life is absent'. Everything I am trying to say here comes down to this: it is up to you to decide that the true life is present. Choose new happiness, and pay the price!

4

Destination and Affects of Philosophy

As we have seen in the preceding chapters, 'happiness' is a synthetic term for diverse affects tied to distinct truth procedures. In *Logics of Worlds* (2006), I indicated explicitly for the first time that the participation of an individual in a truth is signalled by an affect, and that, for each type of truth, there is a different affect. In the present book I opt, finally, for the following denominations: I speak of *enthusiasm* for political action, *beatitude* for scientific discovery, *pleasure* for artistic creation and *joy* for the labour of love. It is true that I have not really described these affects. I have not entered into a phenomenology of their individual value. I will probably attempt to remedy this, partially at least, if I finish writing the third volume of the series whose general title is *Being and Event: The Immanence of Truths*. Among other things, this book bears upon the set of all that happens for a determined individual when incorporated into a truth procedure, when taken up into the Idea. This involves addressing some new points, in particular the distinction of these affects: beatitude is not pleasure, pleasure is not joy, and enthusiasm differs from the other three.

But what is the general need for this third book, after *Being and Event* and *Logics of Worlds*? And in what way does this need bear more particularly on the nature of affects, and thus on the relation between philosophy and the idea of happiness?

Let me first put things in perspective. We can do this simply enough. *Being and Event* can be considered as the first part of a construction in several stages, the part that principally concerns the question of being.[1] What of being, of 'being *qua* being' as Aristotle called it? What are the ways and means of knowing it? My ontological proposition is that being *qua* being is pure multiplicity, that is to say, multiplicity not composed of atoms. Being is evidently composed of elements, but these elements are multiplicities that are themselves composed of multiplicities. However, we arrive at a stopping point, which is not the One – the One would inevitably be an atom – but the void. Such is my proposition on being. As for what we can know of being, my proposition is to identify ontology – the discourse on being – with mathematics, itself considered as the science of the pure multiple, of the multiple 'without qualities' and without One. Moreover, as a counterpoint, *Being and Event* develops a theory of truths, a *formal* theory of truths: truths are, like all things,

---

[1] A. Badiou, *Being and Event*, trans. O. Feltham (London and New York: Continuum, 2005).

multiplicities. Their singularity is that they depend on an event, which is a vanishing multiplicity, a multiplicity that is, within the situation where it takes place, without any foundation. A truth is a multiplicity composed of the consequences of an event, and which is therefore suspended from an unfounded being. It is then a question of knowing what kind of multiplicity it is, paradoxical and quite rare, which we call a truth. The book then traces out both a theory of being and a theory of truths, all within the context of a theory of the pure multiple as it is affected from time to time by an unfounded emergence. From this point of view, the underlying affect of the enterprise – the ontological enterprise – is principally the beatitude engendered by scientific understanding (in this case, the mathematics of multiplicity). Anyone who has had the experience that, in the middle of the night, after many hopeless efforts and scribbled pages, the architecture of a demonstration and the sense it gives to an entire theory is suddenly illuminated, will know what I mean. Beatitude is the name of the happiness that being *qua* being dispenses, once grasped in the writing of its purity.

The second part of this construction, *Logics of Worlds*, sets itself the question of appearing.[2] This is a theory of that which, of being, appears in determined worlds and the formal relations between the objects of these worlds. I call this part of the overall construction a *logic*. It is a logic that no longer bears on the composition of what is, but on the relations that are woven

---

[2] A. Badiou, *Logics of Worlds*, trans. A. Toscano (London and New York: Continuum, 2009).

between all things as they appear locally in worlds. In short, after a theory of being, a theory of *being-there* – to use a vocabulary close to that of Hegel – that is to say, of being such as it is placed and arranged within the relations of a singular world. The underlying affects are undoubtedly the pleasure of the work of art and the joy of love, for the reason that both are profoundly tied to the *jouissance* of one or more relations. In the case of art, the relation with the sensible in all its forms, the different moments of its 'distribution', as Jacques Rancière says; in the case of love, the intimate dialectical experience of difference and its magical power with respect to traversing a world delivered from solitude.

In *Logics of Worlds*, the question of truth is obviously reprised. *Being and Event* treated the being of truths as particular multiplicities, what, after the mathematician Paul Cohen, I have called generic multiplicities. With *Logics of Worlds*, we enter into the question of real bodies, the logic of their relations and in particular the question of the appearing of truths. If all that appears in a world is a body, we must address the question of the body of a truth. This second volume therefore aims broadly at a theory of bodies, which can also be a theory of bodies of truths; whereas the first volume aims at a theory of multiplicities, which is also a theory of truths as multiplicities, generic multiplicities.

That the question of the body of truths is central evidently clarifies that pleasure (of the formalized sensible) and joy (of the other, of the sexed Two as sovereign of the world) are the forms most clearly articulated at this level of happiness.

The third volume of the project examines things, and therefore being and appearing, from *the point of view of truths*. The first volume asks: what are truths in relation to being? The second: what are truths in relation to appearing? The third will ask: what are being and appearing from the point of view of truths? In this way I will have covered the question in its entirety.

The problem is that coming to this third movement involves long detours and very difficult questions.

A truth, from the human point of view, the anthropological point of view, is composed of individual incorporations within larger groups. I would thus like to know how the world and the individuals of the world are presented, how they are positioned, when examined from the interior of truth processes themselves. This is a question that reverses in a way the perspective of the first two volumes. We asked what truths were from the point of being and from the point of view of a world; we now ask what being and the world are from the point of view of truths. Here we encounter problems of scale: truths, like being, are essentially infinite, whereas bodies, such as appear in worlds, seem irremediably marked by finitude. How to present today this dialectic of the finite and the infinite, which has tormented philosophy in its modern epoch since Descartes, for whom, enigmatically, the infinite was an idea 'more clear' than that of the finite?

Obviously, happiness is implicated in this affair, for which a simple definition might be: *all happiness is a finite* jouissance *of the infinite*.

Naturally, there are sketches of this difficulty in the two earlier works. *Being and Event,* in particular, contains a relatively

complicated theory of the return effect of infinite truths working
on the world, following the event that gives rise to them. This
effect resides in the figure of *knowledge*. The thesis is that we will
call knowledge, new knowledge, the creation of a knowledge,
the way in which a truth differently illuminates the ontological
situation. It is as in Plato: we arrive at the Idea by leaving the
cave of appearances, but we must redescend into the cave to
illuminate what exists on the basis of the Idea. And we must
do so, even run a certain number of risks. It is indeed upon
returning to the cave that the risk is greatest, at the moment
when you pronounce, from the point of view of what you
consider to be truths, on the world as it appears, and therefore
on its dominant ideologies. For Plato, only this risk accom-
plishes the Idea, and therefore happiness bound to truth. In
effect, whoever refuses to return to the cave, whoever avoids the
duty of sharing the universality of the true, may well be satisfied
by the possession of the Idea: not the happiness that only this
sharing procures.

I first treated this question of the return in *Being and Event,*
under the name of the *theory of* forcing: you *force* a transformation in common knowledge by participating in a new truth.
It is quite a complex theory, as is already, as a matter of fact, the
theory of the return to the cave in Plato. Plato, ultimately, doesn't
say much about it, except that the return is very risky, very
difficult, as uncertain as it is necessary. Plato tells us that this
return must be forced, since we could stay in the calm domain
of the contemplation of truths where we would have satisfaction,
but would not accede to happiness. Here the term *forcing*, used

in *Being and Event* in terms of the relation of truth to knowledge, is not out of place. It is not a natural or spontaneous procedure. *In a sense, all happiness is obtained by force of will.*

As to *Logics of Worlds*, the book does not contain a theory of forcing, but a theory of the intimate relationship between the singularity of a world and the universality of a truth, traversing the phenomena of concrete, emergent, empirical conditions for the construction of the body of truths. I maintain that the truth is a body. As such, it is made from what there is, that is to say, from other individual bodies, and this is what is called incorporation. This incorporation sheds light on how a truth proceeds in a world and about its relationship with the material of this same world, namely its bodies and language. In *Logics of Worlds*, I begin with the formula: 'In a world, there are only bodies and languages, except that there are truths.' I proceed to a first materialist examination of this 'except that': truths are also bodies and language, subjectivisable bodies. To show the relationship of truths to bodies and to languages, I utilize a notion equivalent to that of forcing in *Being and Event,* namely, the concept of *compatibility.* A body of truths is composed of compatible elements, in a sense both technical and elementary: they let themselves be dominated by the same element.

Basically, a truth is always a unified multiplicity, dominated or organized by something which makes compatible that which is not necessarily so. To take a very simple example, a good part of the conception of what a revolutionary party comprised consisted in creating a theory wherein intellectuals and workers are compatible, and where politics renders compatible class differences which normally are not. Gramsci's theory of the 'organic intellectual' and other neighbouring theories are of this type. These do not simply treat differences of class in terms of conflict. They thus create compatibilities between classes where none have existed: for example, a theory of class alliances. In aesthetics, we have a situation of the same order. A work of art – considered as subject – creates compatibilities between things hitherto considered incompatible, absolutely separated. A painting is created in colours which do not appear destined to go together, between forms that were disparate. It integrates forms and colours in compatibilities of a superior type.

In short, the concept of forcing, at the ontological level, and the concept of compatibility, at the level of phenomenology, already trace the relationship between the truth and the situation in which the truth proceeds and therefore also, implicitly, the new dialectic between the finite and the infinite, which, among other things, is the key to real happiness. The third volume will systematize all this. It will locate itself in some way in the different types of truths in order to ask: What happens when a world is approached from the perspective of a truth? What happens ontologically when we adopt the perspective of generic multiplicities over ordinary multiplicities, which make up any ontological situation? In this context, I will trace out the singular affects which indicate, at the individual level, the processes of incorporation. What is amorous joy? What is aesthetic pleasure? What is political enthusiasm? What is scientific beatitude? In *The Immanence of Truths* all this is studied systematically. I thereby hope to achieve, with the aid of modern theories of the finite and the infinite, a type of speculative science of happiness.

The construction of this coming book can be summed up fairly simply. I set out a broad opening development, more technical and more precise, of the problem I have just briefly introduced: the problem of the relationship between individuals incorporated into a truth and ordinary multiplicities, thought in their being and in their worldly appearing. This task will be organized around a very simple idea, which is that the incorporation of a truth is invariably a new way of articulating the finite dimension of individuals and the infinite dimension of any truth process. The underlying formalism will necessarily be a new dialectic between finite multiplicities and infinite multiplicities, supported by the modern mathematical theory of 'very large infinities'. To my mind, this theory is a crucial requirement for any contemporary philosophy of happiness, among other things because it can distinguish between weak infinities, which can only provide, at best, satisfaction, from strong infinities, on whose occurrence real happiness depends. I envisage a second part, which will clarify the general laws, the formal dispositions, which organize the relations of a world from the point of view of truths. We will have then a general theory of individual incorporation and of its indicative affects. We will ask: What is the clarification of the world from the perspective of truths? What is an obstacle? A victory? A defeat? A creation? A third part will take things truth procedure by truth procedure, proposing a systematic theory of art, science, love and politics. Such a theory, even though an outline of it is evident in various places in my work, is nowhere present. There you have it, the ideal plan of *The Immanence of Truths,* which is actually a *work in progress* [in English in original].

I would like to emphasize that, in the second part, I intend to propose a theory of what the four truth procedures have in common, and of their potential unity. Indeed, this part includes a return to a theory of truths, but this time from the perspective of truths themselves. This will involve asking what these are in themselves, and no longer what differentiates them in the anonymity of their being or as objects of a world. But it will also involve continuing my interrogation of philosophy. As we know, in *Manifesto for Philosophy* I defined it as that which creates a locus of compossibility, a place of coexistence, for the four conditions.[3] It remains to examine whether philosophy does not also rest upon a *figure of life* that would integrate these procedures. It is a question which has been posed to me often enough and I intend to address it head on. Of course we see immediately that all this is what I have already called the true life: but not only this, because, when it is a matter of taking together all four truth procedures, the question is more like: what is a *complete* life? As I said at the close of *Logics of Worlds,* this is the question of the true life. What is the true life, which Rimbaud said was absent, but I maintain can be present? My answer is: it is to live under the sign of the Idea, that is to say, to live under the sign of effective incorporation. The ultimate question in *The Immanence of Truths* is similar, but different: is there an Idea of

---

[3] A. Badiou, *Manifesto for Philosophy,* trans. N. Madarasz (Albany: SUNY, 1999).

ideas, that is to say, an Idea of a complete life? We return thus to the ambition of ancient wisdom. We find this initial aspiration for a life not marked only by the Idea and truth but by the idea of a fulfilled life, a life in which all that can be experienced in the matter of truth has been.

Will this interrogation go so far as to suppose that a philosophical subject can exist? A subject whose affect would be precisely happiness, subsuming under its power pleasure, joy, beatitude and enthusiasm?

The obvious objection is that as it stands so to speak in the middle of the four conditions, which circulates conceptually from art to science to politics and love, it is philosophy itself, and not the subject of philosophy, whose existence is doubtful. The question of the subject will, however, haunt this third volume. I have always resisted the thesis that philosophy was itself a truth procedure like the others. It cannot be like the others, since it depends on their existence, whereas neither art nor science nor love nor politics depends on the existence of philosophy. It is therefore obvious that philosophy is out of sync in relation to the four types of truth procedure. Nevertheless, the question of knowing whether we can indicate the place of a philosophical subject is an open one. If there is a philosophical subject, what is it like? What is it that has access to philosophy? What is it to be in philosophy? There is certainly no philosophical incorporation in the sense found in the political militant, the artist, the scientist or lover. And yet one has access, in philosophy, to a consistent thought, and not to nothing. The question remains open. If we suppose the existence of a subject of philosophy, what would be its place? Is it, as some of my metaphors suggest, an absent centre? It is clear that philosophy proposes a general doctrine of a subject of truth. But how do we enter into this philosophical proposition, what nurtures us there? What new method permits its return to the truth procedures? How, finally, can it open the way to the true life or the complete life? These are the questions I ask. It is clear that my approach to these questions has always been somewhat hesitant. I am confronted by an unresolved problem. That my philosophy is systematic is not to pretend it has resolved all problems!

It must be said that up until now I have had a tendency to address certain problems negatively, by rejecting rather than proposing them. Thus I have rejected the sophistic thesis according to which philosophy is only a general unification of things because it is a general rhetoric. The linguistic turn of the twentieth century basically resulted in a type of doctrine that assimilates philosophy to a general rhetoric. This can go as far as Barbara Cassin's thesis: there is no ontology, only a logology. It is language that cuts out and constitutes all that is proposed as the form of being. The twentieth century has known a tendency, at once academic, critical, anti-dogmatic, which progressively centred on the creative power of language. Derrida was the subtle master of this tendency. In my view, this makes philosophy into a general rhetoric, an inventive, modern rhetoric, all that you could want. But, as I have said many times, I am not in this register. In the dispute between Plato and the sophists I am without hesitation on the side of Plato, the Plato of the *Cratylus*, for whom, as we have seen, philosophy begins with things and not words. We, the philosophers, begin with things and not words. I add here that the doctrine of the sophists is a theory of satisfaction, not a theory of happiness. And this is because it is resigned to finitude, knowing nothing of the infinite.

Thus, negatively, I have already taken a series of positions on the access to philosophy, and on the role of that access in this latest question of happiness. On a more affirmative note, I designated what I called philosophical operations: I therefore spoke of operations, not events. Two of them seem to me impossible to contest. In the first place, the operations of identification: philosophy signposts truths, in particular the truths of its time, through the construction of a renewed concept of what a truth is. Second operation: through the category of truth, philosophy makes compossible different and heterogeneous registers of truth. There is a function of discernment and a function of unification. Philosophy has always been held between the two. Discernment leads to a critical conception, the distinction of what is true and not true; unification leads to different usages of the categories of totality and of system.

I maintain these two classical functions of philosophy. I have always affirmed that I was classical. I show that philosophy elaborates, contemporaneously with its conditions, the categories of truth that allow it to discern these conditions, to isolate them, and to show they are not reducible to the way of the ordinary world. It also tries to think in some way a concept of the contemporary, indicating how the conditions comprise an epoch, a dynamics of thought, in which every subject is inscribed. In this sense, philosophy designates the possible horizon of any true happiness.

But we must go further and ask about the relationship of philosophy to life. It is a fundamental question. If we cannot say that the perspective of philosophy is that of the true life, then it is just another academic discipline. The third volume therefore also attempts to create the possibility of confronting this question. This will take up again the Platonic question of the relationship of philosophy and happiness.

In sum, we will pass from a negative doctrine of the universal singularity of truths to an immanent and affirmative doctrine. I am myself struck by the fact that I have so far treated truths, and consequently the subject – the subject is the protocol of orientation for a truth, truth and subject are bound absolutely – only in a differential manner. I asked what type of multiplicity a truth is. What differentiates it from some other multiple? This was the fundamental proposition of *Being and Event*. Thus, at the time I was already in the exception. If a truth is an exception to the laws of the world, we need to explain in what this exception consists. If we are in the domain of ontology, the theory of being, the mathematical theory of being, we should be able to explain mathematically the type of multiplicity that singularises truths. Relying on set theory and the theorems of Cohen, I show that this multiplicity is *generic*. In other words, it is a multiplicity which does not let itself be thought by the knowledges available. No predicate of available knowledge permits its identification. This is what Cohen's technique serves: to show that an indiscernible multiplicity can exist, which doesn't allow itself to be discerned by the predicates that circulate in these knowledges. In this way, truth escapes knowledge at the level of its being. This appears to be a positive determination of truths: they are generic multiplicities. But on closer inspection this is a negative determination: these are multiplicities that *are not* reducible to available knowledge. My definition of truth therefore passes through a differential approach, and not through an intrinsic or immanent construction.

In *Logics of Worlds*, truth is defined as a subjectivizable body. What are its specific characteristics? There are many, but one is central: the protocol for the construction of this body is that all that composes it is compatible. Nevertheless, this compatibility is only a relational characteristic of a truth. Within any truth we find a relation of compatibility between all its elements. This is an objective characteristic. In both cases, I have therefore arrived at a precise objective determination: for the being of a truth and for the appearing of a truth, respectively, the concepts of genericity and compatibility. But a subjective determination is, precisely, lacking. None of this tells us what a truth is as experienced from the interior of a truth procedure, that is to say, what it is for the subject of truth itself.

My responses to these questions remain, in my opinion, overly functional. Ontologically, I say that the subject is a point, a local instant of a truth. Phenomenologically, I say that it is the function of orientation for the construction of a subjectivizable body. These are functional definitions, which themselves remain objective. It is necessary, now, to have something that materializes, writes, organizes the protocol of truth, this time seen in an immanent fashion, that is to say *subjectivity* as such. In *Theory of the Subject,* I distinguished the 'subjective process' and 'subjectivization'.[4] To utilize this distinction, I would say *Being and Event* and *Logics of Worlds* contain something decisive concerning the 'subjective process', but that 'subjectivization' remains obscure, treated negatively and in a purely differential manner. Subjectivization is the way in which one subjectivizes the protocol of truth from within. It lacks an intuition of what a subjectivization is. But, as I have said many times in this book, happiness is decisively linked to subjectivization.

But how do we speak convincingly of subjectivization? And what are the formal protocols of such a treatment? At least for the moment, I know one thing: it will entail a formal transformation of the category of negation. In particular, it will suppose we can have simultaneously a 'strong' negation (in the Marxist political tradition we say: an antagonistic or 'irreconcilable' contradiction) and a 'weak' negation, which admits of non-destructive contradictions, of contradictions that do not entail the putting-to-death of one of the two terms.

It is in line with such a concept that we must make use of new formalizations. If the subjective protocols of a truth are composed of assemblies or of incorporations of individuals in the becoming of a truth, the question is then of knowing how individuated difference functions within the truth protocol. This is a question which has always interested me. Consider a

---

[4] A. Badiou, *Theory of the Subject*, trans. with intro. B. Bosteels (London: Continuum, 2009).

very simple example. Two people are looking at a picture. We have a fragment of incorporation, a fragment signalled by a certain affect, by a work of intelligence, by the immobilization of the gaze on the picture. I place myself in the point of view of the spectator rather than the creator, to indicate that a truth is constantly available for incorporation. Is this act of subjectivization, which is incorporation, identical for both spectators? Is it a matter of identity or compatibility? In any case, we cannot say that the duality at the heart of this experience – an experience which can be had by millions of people – will rupture the unity of the subject. How is this possible? Much of the scepticism with regard to truths is rooted in this type of experience. To each his truth, said Pirandello. 'To each his truth' implies that there is no truth at all. In the case of a picture, there is a unique object which is dislocated according to the various perceptions. We could say that pleasure, the synthetic form of happiness in artistic contemplation, is dispersed in many disjunct satisfactions.

Now, why does this problem of subjective dispersion concern negation? Because the difficulty is knowing on what type of negation this dispersion turns. Everyone sees the picture in their own way, the perception of one *is not* the perception of the other. But what does 'is not' signify? That which dislocates perception and leads to scepticism is the idea that this 'is not' is a classical negation, that is to say that one of the perceptions can and must be in contradiction with the other.

On what theory of negation can we rely in order to avoid this sceptical consequence of ordinary negation? The answer must be based on the paraconsistent theory of negation, the third type of logic (after classical and intuitionist) discovered by the Brazilian Da Costa, for which the principle of non-contradiction is not valid. Besides the detailed use of the theory of infinity, the new formalism this third book will introduce on a large scale is paraconsistent negation, which explicitly contradicts the principle of non-contradiction. This formalism allows, when considering a truth, for contradictory perceptions to co-exist without interrupting the unity of this truth. What is of great interest to me is that a problem of this kind is posed at the heart of love; if we allow – this is my thesis, that we must accept, for a complete understanding – the coexistence of the feminine position and the masculine position; positions that in certain regards are entirely disjunct.

If the major formalism of *Being and Event* was set theory and Cohen's theorem, if the major formalism of *Logics of Worlds* was the theory of sheaves, topology, and therefore broadly an intuitionist logic, the formalism of this third volume will be the relating of the modern theory of the infinite and paraconsistent logic, with a meditation on the limits of the principle of non-contradiction. We could say that happiness is simultaneously an intra-finite subjectivization of the infinite, and that it is divided, in the sense that my subjectivization 'is not' that of the other, without for all that contradicting it, since negation is here paraconsistent.

However, there are not only the formalisms: in fact, they are only a sort of scaffolding for the conceptual construction and they assume a good dose of intuition. Arguably, every philosopher experiences a subjective contact with the truth

– his personal point of encounter with a truth in some way. It is this point he tries to transmit through his philosophy. But, at the same time, he knows, deep down inside himself, that this point is not transmissible, being absolutely his own contact with truth. Would this not explain, in particular, the difficulty Plato experienced in defining the Idea of the Good? Do we not risk at this point, arriving at the ineffable? This is the product of many philosophical dispositions. We end up with a point that is the ultimate point of the real. The latter, conforming to what Lacan says, is that which cannot be symbolized. Spinoza, for example, names this ultimate point the intellectual intuition of God, but he gives no real intuition of it. The proof is that its best approximation is the beatitude attested by mathematical knowledge. Yet mathematical knowledge is the second kind of understanding, not the third. The intuition of the ultimate point thus escapes. As for Plato, in the *Republic* he expressly declares that he can give only an image of the Good, and nothing else.

The *Immanence of Truths* will in part be an attempt to maximally circumscribe this point, with the hope of reducing its ineffability. It is a question of making it as minimally ineffable as possible, and therefore also as transmissible as possible. As yet I do not know how far I will have to go in this direction. But I know that I break here, to my great regret, with Plato.

Plato starts from a philosophical experience of the Idea, but the necessity of transmitting this experience remains for him largely exterior to the content of the experience itself. This is why he affirms that it is necessary to force philosophers to become politicians and educators. When they have been brought to the Idea of the Good, their only idea is to stay there. The necessity of transmission, which comes from outside the very experience of the truth, is for Plato a social and political requirement. It is necessary that this experience can be shared at the level of the general organization of society. If we have no such transmission, we leave people in the empire of dominant opinions. We must therefore 'corrupt' the youth, in the sense of Socrates, that is, by transmitting the means to not be enslaved by dominant opinions.

I share entirely this vision of philosophy. And I am very attached, as you know, to its didactic. But we must recognize that in Plato there is an obscurity with regard to the question of knowing the nature of truth. Of this truth, he does not truly speak. We know that there are absolutely contradictory interpretations of Plato. He could be seen by Galileo, and many others, as the epitome of scientific rationalism. But for the Neoplatonists he was the epitome of transcendent theology. These divergences are explained by the fact that Plato said little about the truth of which he spoke. In some way, he withheld the experience. And perhaps, to go further, he lacked a rationalization of the concept of infinity, its mathematical pluralization, for which humanity had to wait for more than two millennia, between Eudoxus and Cantor. For it is very difficult to think what a truth is without being able to say clearly that it partakes of a type of infinity different from that in which it operates, or is constructed, and that the true-infinite is not the infinite-that-is. This is also why the Platonic theory of happiness, correct in principle (happiness is the subjectivization of the true) remains abstract as to its possibility.

For me, as I characterize them, truths exist. I have said so and will say explicitly how and why they exist. It is true that transmission is difficult here. What is to be transmitted is that truths, insofar as they exist, are, firstly, exceptional to the rest, and, secondly, exist as works, on the basis of a tight dialectic between various types of infinity. Plato also presents his Idea of the Good as exceptional. The idea of the Good is not an Idea! According to a passage in the *Republic* often commented on, it far exceeds the Idea in power and prestige. What can this be? Negative theology says it is God, and of God we can say nothing. On the rationalist side we find the interpretation of Monique Dixsaut and many others – mine also, as it happens. It consists in showing that there is a principle of intelligibility which is not reducible to the Idea itself. The Idea, as principle of intelligibility, is naturally situated beyond the Idea as local principle of action or creation. Undoubtedly, Plato did not possess the means – infinites of a higher kind and paraconsistent logic – to conceptualize this 'beyond'.

Plato is a foundational figure and of very great importance to me. But we have to acknowledge that he is evasive. He shows an obliqueness, which the dialogue form moreover favours, because we never know exactly who speaks and who tells the truth. It flows like a torrent: at the end, we have understood the problem, but not its solution. We don't know exactly in what sense Plato has spoken. It's a bit of an organized disappointment. For example, the interlocutors of Socrates, in the *Republic*, point out that it is high time he define this Idea of the Good that he has maintained for so long. We then see how Socrates deals with it, and he says something like: 'you ask too much of me!'

This is not my style. On the contrary, I try to say the maximum that can be said. I am a more affirmative and less evasive Platonist than Plato. At least, I try! This is my conception of philosophy: an exercise in the transmission of something we could just as well declare impossible to transmit. In this sense, then, it is the impossible proper to philosophy, its purpose, its end. I am therefore engaged in a struggle against contemporary scepticism, cultural relativism, generalized rhetoric, exactly as Plato was engaged against the sophists. My position is the affirmation of truth as exception, but not thereby declaring it intransmissible, because that would demonstrate a considerable weakness in the face of the dominant nihilism.

However, I leave open the possibility that the concept of truth, and further, that which I call its ideation, meaning the incorporation of an individual into the becoming of a truth, is, as appears to be the case in Plato, not easily transmissible. With regard to this, it is interesting to consider the programme of philosophical apprenticeship in the *Republic*: 1. Arithmetic: 2. Geometry: 3. Spatial geometry: 4. Astronomy: 5. Dialectic. Yet, as everyone can see, in the passage on the dialectic there is almost nothing! It is enough, then, to register that the philosophical apprenticeship is basically in mathematics and astronomy, thus referring explicitly to a scientific condition. Beyond this foundation, 'dialectic' names something different. But this difference remains abstract: it is not any clearer than the Idea of the Good. We are thus tempted to reduce happiness to mathematical beatitude. But this I cannot do.

Must we then go along with Bergson's famous thesis that every philosopher becomes conscious of an ungraspable point? As he says: 'In this point is something simple, infinitely simple, so extraordinarily simple that the philosopher has never succeeded in saying it. And that is why he went on talking all his life'.[5]

If I can see a point of this type in my philosophy, it is definitively that of happiness. I have discerned and identified that it consists in thinking the subjectivization of the true right to the end – and not only the existence of truth processes. This is what I call incorporation, not grasped in its objective logic, but regrasped from the point of view of the individual itself, in the moment where it partakes in the activity of a Subject, because it is incorporated into the becoming-body of truth. The intuition of this incorporation is accompanied in general by a singular affect, which is, without doubt, nothing other than this feeling of difficulty in transmitting that of which we speak. This problem will be the object of my forthcoming work, undoubtedly my last.

Yet I am hesitant to say that the obstacle is simplicity. Such simplicity is evidently typical of Bergsonian ontology, an ontology that is not mathematical but vitalist. The radical point of vitalist ontology consists in situating itself in the pure differential of movement or duration. This is indeed where we can have the experience of absolute simplicity and at the same time locate the foundation of thought for Bergson. But when the ontology is mathematical, as in my case, we start from an

---

[5] H. Bergson, *The Creative Mind: An Introduction to Metaphysics*, trans. M. L. Andison (New York: Dover, 2007), pp. 88–9.

intrinsic complexity, a pure multiplicity, which doesn't refer to an originary simplicity other than the void. It goes without saying: of the void, we can say nothing more.

Finally, I agree with Bergson that there is an originary point of experience, a point that any philosophical didactics struggles to answer and transmit. But I think that the experience of this point is the concentrated experience of a complexity and not the experience of a simplicity. I find myself, instead, in agreement with Spinoza: the example he proposes for the third kind of knowledge, intuitive and absolute knowledge, is of a mathematical demonstration that would be picked up in a point. This suits me. When we have truly understood a mathematical demonstration, we no longer need the steps; we have understood something that is gathered in a point. That said, the didactic is obliged to retrace the steps, because there is a complexity at this point, a hidden complexity, to the extent that we are dealing with a point. It is not the same thing to have a contracted complexity, and a pure simplicity as with Bergson. Therefore, happiness is not, as it is for a vitalist, in the simplicity of impetus [*l'élan*], but in the secret complexity of the ideal point which guides our incorporation into the true, whether it be the political masses, amorous duality, mathematical algorithms, or the formalisms of the sensible.

Rather than vitalist, I believe I am at once materialist and Platonist. I can pick up here on a striking fact. Althusser himself argued, with particular force, the idea that the principal contradiction in philosophy was between materialism and idealism. However to follow this thesis through within the conditions of modern materialism, taking into account mathematics, modern science, the general appraisal of materialism, he was constrained to introduce the concept of *aleatory materialism*. For very many reasons, it is necessary to make the question of chance inevitable for any contemporary materialism, the most spectacular of those reasons being the development of quantum mechanics. In the unity of the materialist schema I develop, the objective existence of multiplicities is bordered, so to speak, by the possibility of the aleatory, by the possibility that something happens which can be neither foreseen, nor calculated, nor reincorporated from the existing state of things. This is what I call an event. There is something like a hazardous absolute point, hazardous in the sense that it doesn't allow itself to be organized by that from which it proceeds. I need nothing other than this hazardous point. An event suffices for me to deploy the truth as exception. And I do not depart from materialism, which has no intrinsic reason to be organically linked to determinism. Determinism was only one of the possible conceptions of materialism.

As we have known since the origins of materialism, determinism is insufficient, since, in primitive atomism, the *clinamen*, that sudden atomic deviation, without place or cause, introduces an event subtracted from all determination – which I spoke of at length in *Theory of the Subject*. I admire in particular the first, consequential, heroic materialists – Democritus, Epicurus, Lucretius – who, in a world of gods and superstitions, introduced the radical thesis that there are only atoms and the void. However, faced with this evidence, they couldn't deduce the event from the world of atoms and the void alone. There had to be a third term, which is the form of pure chance. Finally, when I say: 'There are only bodies and languages, except that there are truths', I accomplish an Epicurean gesture. I say that there is an exception. But this exception is itself founded only on the existence of the event. And the event is nothing other than the possibility of the aleatory in the structure of the world. I don't at all think that with the introduction of events I leave materialism. Some have adjudged that this was a new dualism. I was told: 'You introduce the exception, it's no longer materialism.' But it is the case that the consequences of an exception are entirely situated within a world. There is not a sensible schema and an intelligible schema, a schema of the event and a schema of the world, which would be distinct. I also maintain that we can interpret Plato by avoiding this duality of the sensible and the intelligible, which are the resort of vulgar Platonism. Certainly, Plato often expresses himself like this. But don't forget his evasiveness, cunning, and the very frequent use of images.

To return to the event, to the aleatory, is to insist on the existence of a break. There is a before and after. This break is not the passage from an inferior world to a superior world. We are always in the same world. The consequences of the break certainly have an exceptional status in relation to what does not depend upon the break. But we have to show that these consequences are organized according to the general logic of the world itself. It is a demonstration, a labour I impose on myself every time. My Old Marxist friends, such as the late Daniel Bensaïd, who accuse me of having introduced a miraculous element, are simply mechanistic materialists. Already, Marx, and even Lucretius, squared off against them.

Let us add that, when you are a non-mechanistic materialist, you are a dialectician. Indeed, I believe that my philosophical enterprise can be considered a vast traversal of the dialectic. I have maintained, from beginning to end, the idea that the ontological status of truths has the status of an exception: a generic exception in relation to that which is constructible; an exception of subjectivizable bodies in relation to ordinary bodies; the exception of my materialism in relation to a simplistic materialism, for which there are only bodies and languages. But the category of exception is a dialectical category, the thought of the exception always taking place on two contradictory sides. We must think exception as a negation, since it is not reducible to the ordinary, but we must also not think of it as a miracle. We must therefore think it as internal to the process of a truth – not miraculous – and, despite this, still think it as exception. This is, after all, the evidence of happiness. On the one side, it is like a present that the world makes us, for us, individuals on the way to becoming subjects. But, on the other side, this present is supernumerary, improbable, exceptional, albeit made of nothing other than the material of the world. It is the finally experienced latent infinity of all finitude, without which this infinity would be transcendent. On the contrary, it is the most profound immanence.

This might be what Lacan wanted to signify by 'extimacy': at once intimate and exterior to the intimate. Now we are within the kernel of the dialectic. In Hegel, for example, the negation of a thing is immanent to that thing, but at the same time exceeds it. The kernel of the dialectic is this status of negation, as an operator which separates and includes at the same time. In this sense, I would say that I am continuously in the dialectic, and especially in *Theory of the Subject*, a book still closely linked to classical Marxism and its Maoist developments. In *Theory of the Subject*, there is no general theory of the four conditions of philosophy; any more than there is a general theory of the event. The fundamental categories of *Being and Event* are only implicit there, just as what would support their unification remains somewhat fragmentary. But we can say that I pursue throughout my philosophical enterprise – from *Theory of the Subject*, thirty-two years ago, to the future, *The Immanence of Truths* – a meditation on negation. I am simply trying to account for the possibility of change, of the possibility of passing from a certain regime of the laws of what is, to another regime, by the mediation of the protocol of a truth and its subject. Thus I am in dialectical thought, and in a dialectical theory of happiness, which is the paraconsistent negation of finitude by a complete infinite. But as my thought of the dialectic includes a figure of chance, it is non-deterministic. Recall that the Hegelian dialectic is implacably determinist. As such, it is a typically grand thought of the nineteenth century. It is the spectacle of the self-development of the Absolute in the immanent necessity of its development. I am clearly very far from all this. This is why my relationship to Hegel is close and complicated at the same time. We mustn't forget that, in my three great books already published, Hegel is meticulously discussed: in *Theory of the Subject*, concerning the dialectic itself; in *Being and Event*, concerning the infinite; in *Logics of Worlds*, concerning being-there, the categories of being-there. In *Immanence of Truths*, I will mainly discuss the Hegelian concept of the Absolute, because ultimately, for me, as with Hegel or Plato, all real happiness is a sort of provisional access to the Absolute. Except that our ideas on this question are not the same. I have always been in close discussion with Hegel, but also with Marx, Lenin and Mao, the great revolutionary dialecticians, regarding the political condition. Simply, by the presence of an aleatory element, I introduce a principle of the break that is not exactly homogenous with the classical principles of negation. This is why, finally, I utilize three different and intertwined logics: classical logic, intuitionist logic and paraconsistent logic. And at the same time I elevate the ontological referent to the absolute – the thought of the pure multiple – by way of the theory, truly sensational, of 'very large infinities'. A logical triple and the infinity of infinities will be the key to a general theory of happiness, which is the goal of every philosophy.

Philosophy, for me, is that discipline of thought, that singular discipline, which begins with the conviction that there are truths. From there, it is led to an imperative, a vision of life. What is this vision? What has value for a human individual, what delivers him to a true life and orients his existence, is to participate in these truths. This supposes the very complicated construction of an apparatus to discern truths, an apparatus which allows circulation among them, of compossibilizing them. All this in the mode of contemporaneity.

Philosophy is this path. Thus it goes from life, which proposes the existence of truths, to the life that makes of this existence a principle, a norm, an experience. What are we given by the epoch we live in? What is it? What are the things that have value? What are the things that don't have value? Philosophy proposes to sort through the confusion of experience, from which it draws an orientation. This raising of confusion to another level is the philosophical operation par excellence, and its proper didactic.

This implies a concept of truth. This 'truth' can very well take on another name. Thus, in part of Deleuze's work what we call 'truth' is called 'sense'. I can identify in any philosophy what I would myself call 'truth'. It can be named 'Good', 'spirit', 'active force', 'noumenon' … I choose 'truth' because I am a classicist.

We therefore have to sort, and for this we need a sorting machine; which is to say a concept of truth. We must show that this truth truly exists, but that it is not a miracle and thus that there is no need of a transcendent apparatus. Some philosophies hold to these transcendent apparatus. But that is not my way. I come back to the simple, initial question: What is it to live? What is a worthy and intense life, one not reducible to strict animal parameters? A life which signifies the affect here in question, the affect of real happiness?

I think philosophy must include, in both its conceptions and its propositions, the conviction that the true life can be experienced immanently. Something must signify true life from its own interior, not only as an exterior imperative, as a Kantian imperative. This is part of an affect which signals, indicates, immanently, that life is worth living. There is in Aristotle a formula I like very much and happily repeat: 'Live as an immortal'. There are other names for this affect: 'beatitude' in Spinoza, 'joy' in Pascal, 'overman' in Nietzsche, 'holiness' in Bergson, 'respect' in Kant … I believe that there is an affect of the true life, and I give it the very simple name *happiness*. This affect has no sacrificial component. Nothing negative is required. There is not, as in religions, a sacrifice whose reward is tomorrow and elsewhere. This affect is the affirmative feeling of an expansion of the individual, since it co-belongs to the subject of a truth.

I realized only recently the incredible obstinacy of Plato's demonstration that the philosopher is happy. The philosopher is happier than those who believe they are happier than he is, the rich, the hedonists, the tyrants … Plato incessantly returns to this. He gives us innumerable demonstrations of this point: someone is only truly happy if they live under the sign of the Idea, and is the happiest of all. What this means is clear enough: the philosopher experiences, from within his life, that which is the true life.

Philosophy is three things. It is a diagnosis of the epoch: what does the epoch propose? It is a construction, on the basis of this contemporary proposition, of a concept of truth. It is, finally, an existential experience relative to the true life. Philosophy is the unity of the three. But, at any given moment, philosophy is *a* philosophy. When I have written *The Immanence of Truths*, having thus truly proposed the unity of the three components of any philosophy, I will be able to say: philosophy is me. And it is also, equally, all of you, who read me, and think with me, or against me as well. For if there is thought, there is also the eternity of an earthly experience, that of an immanence to the true life. Then, all of us, friends and enemies, will share the happiness of this immanence.

Conclusion

Throughout this book, definitions of happiness have been proposed, contested, tested, rejected, accepted … Below, in the guise of a recapitulation of my trajectory, twenty of these definitions, accompanied by the page number where they figure.

1   Happiness is the infallible sign of all access to truth (p. 35).

2   Happiness is not the reward of virtue, but virtue itself [Spinoza] (p. 35).

3   Happiness is the affirmative experience of an interruption of finitude (p. 38).

4   Happiness is the affect of the true life (p. 36).

5   Real happiness is a subjective figure of the Open (p. 47).

6   Real happiness is the affect of democracy (p. 48).

7   Real happiness is the *jouissance* of new forms of life (p. 49).

8   All real happiness supposes a liberation of time (p. 59).

9   There is happiness only for what of an individual consents to becoming subject (p. 64).

10　Operating under the imperative of the true Idea destines us to happiness (p. 66).

11　All real happiness plays out in a contingent encounter, there is no necessity to be happy (p. 71).

12　A certain dose of despair is the condition of real happiness (p. 72).

13　The affect of the effect of the subject, whether political enthusiasm, scientific beatitude, aesthetic pleasure or the joy of love, is always what merits, beyond all satisfaction of needs, the name of happiness (p. 73).

14　Happiness is always the *jouissance* of the impossible (p. 85).

15　All real happiness is a fidelity (p. 85).

16　Happiness is the advent, in an individual, of the Subject that it discovers it can become (p. 85).

17　Happiness is the affect of the Subject as immanent exception (p. 85).

18　The true essence of freedom, essential condition of real happiness, is discipline (p. 86).

19　All happiness is a victory against finitude (p. 87).

20　All happiness is a finite *jouissance* of the infinite (p. 95).

Index of Names